How to Raise an Ox

How to Raise an Ox

Zen Practice
As Taught
in Master
Dogen's
Shobogenzo

by
Francis Dojun Cook

Foreword by Taizan
Maezumi Roshi

WISDOM PUBLICATIONS • BOSTON

Wisdom Publications
199 Elm Street
Somerville, MA 02144 USA
www.wisdompubs.org

Library of Congress Cataloging-in-Publication Data
Cook, Francis Harold, 1930–
    How to raise an ox : Zen practices as taught in Zen master
Dōgen's Shōbōgenzō / by Francis Dojun Cook ; foreword by
Taizan Maezumi Roshi.
        p. cm.
    Originally published: Los Angeles : Center Publications, 1978.
    Includes index.
    ISBN 0-86171-317-6
    1. Dōgen, 1200–1253. Shōbōgenzō. 2. Spiritual life—Sōtōshū.
3. Sōtōshū—Doctrines. I. Dōgen, 1200–1253. Shōbōgenzō.
Selections. English. 2002. II. Title.
BQ9449.D654S S53325 2002
294.3'444—dc21   2002001353

ISBN 0-86171-317-6

First Wisdom Edition
07
6   5   4   3   2

Cover design by Richard Snizik
Interior design by Gopa & Ted2
Cover photo by Akira Kaede/Photodisc

Contents

THE ZEN MASTER YÜAN-CHIH of Chang-ching Hall in Fu country once addressed the monks in the Dharma hall: "For thirty years I lived on Mount Wei and during that time I ate the monastery's rice and gave it back in the latrine. I did not learn the Zen of Master Wei-shan. All I did was raise an ox. When he wandered from the path into the grass, I pulled him back; when he ran amuck in someone's garden, I chastised him with a whip. Now he has been tame for some time. Unfortunately, he used to pay too much attention to what people said; now, however, he has become a pure white domesticated ox. He is always right in front of me wherever I am, dazzling white all day long, and even if I try to drive him away, he will not go." We should pay careful attention to this story. The thirty years of arduous practice with Wei-shan consisted of eating rice, and there was no other consideration. When you realize the meaning of the life of eating rice, you will also understand the deep meaning of raising the ox.

Zen Master Dōgen,
from *Shōbōgenzō Kajō*

IT CAN BE SAID that the writings of Dōgen are among the highest achievements not only of Japanese literature but even of world literature. The esteem in which his work is held stems at least in part from its multiple levels of purpose and meaning. When we appreciate his work as literature, it displays true poetic mastery, and yet many of his essays serve admirably as criticism. Viewed philosophically, Dōgen's writings are a near-perfect expression of truth; while from a moral and ethical standpoint, we see beautifully expressed the absolute goodness and righteousness of which the human race is capable. Perhaps most cogently, as a body of religious work we see in these writings that excellent state of well-accomplished enlightenment that far transcends the duality of good and evil.

Dōgen's expression is like an inexhaustible spring that gushes out of the ground naturally and without impediment. Indeed, so freely does his wisdom spring forth that readers often feel almost lost as they read, nearly drowning in that fountain's endless flow.

Amid such richness and subtlety, the task of translation and interpretation might overwhelm most scholars, both Eastern and Western. The demands of Dōgen's language and insight are indeed rigorous, and present formidable challenges to translator and interpreter alike.

It is most fortunate that Dr. Cook has done the work contained in this volume. Highly respected in academic and scholarly circles for his masterful command of the Japanese language, he also has been devotedly practicing Zen meditation for many years. Dr. Cook's practice affords him an experiential base from which he can speak with considerable authority. Going beyond the mere intellectualizing and speculation that so sharply limit much contemporary Zen scholarship, his translations and interpretations can be solidly relied upon by both scholar and practitioner.

He has chosen well from the ninety-five chapters of Dōgen's masterwork, the *Shōbōgenzō,* to present some of the central aspects of Zen practice as Dōgen experienced and transmitted it.

I shall not attempt to add to what he has already expressed so well in the first half of this book. Rather, I should like to encourage readers themselves to personally experience, interpret, and evaluate what Dr. Cook says in this excellent translation and interpretation of Dōgen's work. Then, having read about how to raise an ox, the next step, naturally, is to raise one.

Hakuyu Taizan Maezumi
Los Angeles
September, 1978

Preface

My FUNCTION in bringing these chapters of the *Shōbōgenzō* to the attention of Western readers has been merely that of a kind of midwife. The splendor and beauty of the baby is not at all my doing but is the contribution of the mother. I offer this volume in the hope that my fellow Westerners will come to appreciate the magnificent work of Dōgen as I have. My primary objective is to help the reader to gain a better understanding of what it means to practice Zen, particularly in the Sōtō form that Dōgen established.

Far from hindering the study of the right kind of literature, Zen practice can contribute greatly to it. In learning to apply zazen to everyday life—which is one of the most important features of Zen training—everything one does comes to be zazen. This applies to reading and study too, if, of course, the literature is not trivial or distracting. In the world of Zen training, where there is ultimately neither good nor bad, reading and study are no better or worse than any other activity. The notion that reading is bad for one's spiritual health is the result of a misunderstanding of the relationship between Zen and literary activity. Zen should not be used as an excuse for sloppiness or laziness in study or any other endeavor. In fact, the library was an important part of Zen monastic compounds in Chinese Buddhism, and Dōgen included a library in his own monastery, Eiheiji. He also wrote a list of monastic rules, called *shingi,* that prescribe in minute detail how one should comport oneself in the monastery, and among which are many rules that have to do with respect for books. The right literature—and the *Shōbōgenzō* is surely included in this category—can do much to clarify what practice is and is not, point out dangerous pitfalls, and most of all, inspire one to practice diligently. Each of us needs this constant inspiration to practice in the very best way we can. A work such as the *Shōbōgenzō*, in its discussion of Zen practice, in its examples of great Zen masters, and particularly in the example of the mind of Dōgen himself, offers us one of the very finest sources for this inspiration and encouragement. Surely anyone who reads what Dōgen has to say about Zen practice will perceive some of Dōgen's spirit and without a doubt be encouraged by it.

—F.D.C.

Introduction

THE ZEN OF Dōgen is the Zen of practice. Whatever else may be said about the ninety-five chapters of his *Shōbōgenzō*—and there is so much that has been said!—it is clear that the main theme that runs through these chapters is that of the necessity for daily, diligent, and continuous practice of Zen. To understand what it means to say that Dōgen's Zen is the Zen of practice is to understand something of that remarkable man's place in the development of Buddhism, as well as something of the nature of Buddhism itself. It is my earnest hope that these translations of nine chapters from *Shōbōgenzō* and of *Fukan zazengi* will help to clarify for us Dōgen's Zen of practice.

Western students of Buddhism these days are perhaps not quite so prone to making the same errors of interpretation that characterized earlier generations, but there still remains a tendency to misunderstand certain aspects of Buddhism. For instance, it is generally said that the goal of Buddhism is enlightenment. In a sense, this is true, but it is misleading when it is claimed without qualification; it might be more accurate to say that in Mahayana Buddhism, enlightenment is the doorway through which one must necessarily pass in order to reach the *true* goal. Enlightenment is sometimes imagined as a sudden, dramatic, transformational event that occurs only after a long preparatory period of moral self-cleansing and hard meditation, the prize that is finally claimed after much practice, and that is the culmination and termination of that practice. For if practice exists for the sake of enlightenment, why practice once the prize is won? Yet this is precisely what Dōgen and the masters of old did.

They tell us repeatedly that there is nothing to attain. But in reality, this "nothing" is attained many times and in varying degrees of intensity and depth.

To characterize Dōgen's Zen as the Zen of practice is not to suggest that his form of Buddhism is the only one concerned with practice. All forms of Buddhism necessarily involve some kind of practice because Buddhism *is* mainly practice. Buddhism is a markedly experiential religion inasmuch as the true life in the Dharma involves a realization (i.e., a making real) of those doctrines taught by Shakyamuni, and this making real does not happen in the absence of constant effort—the continual and conscious direction of the will toward realization. Without this effort, Buddhism would degenerate into mere philosophy, into a mechanical profession of faith, or into vague, warm feelings directed toward some remote, mysterious Other.

Dōgen's unique Zen of practice can be seen clearly in certain phrases in the *Shōbōgenzō*. *Honshō myōshū* means "wonderful practice based on intrinsic enlightenment." It is an important phrase because it embodies two ideas that are central to Dōgen's understanding of Buddhism. *Honshō* ("intrinsic enlightenment") refers to the idea that all living beings are already Buddhas. This does not mean that beings *possess* a Buddha nature, or that beings are containers in which a seed form of Buddha can be found, as if there were two realities: beings and Buddha. All beings are Buddhas, but they are Buddhas who are ignorant of their true nature. Second, the whole phrase, *honshō myōshū,* points to the manner in which beings should proceed to make this hidden nature manifest and functional. Practice should not be undertaken in the mistaken notion that it has a purely instrumental value, as a means to a separate—and presumably greater!—end. To believe that one does zazen *now* in order to acquire enlightenment *later* is to merely perpetuate the very dualities that lie at the root of the human problem. This mistaken view tacitly assumes that there is a difference between beings and Buddha, means and ends, now and then—and thus practice becomes just one more attempt to achieve ego-gratification. The belief that practice *culminates* in enlightenment is a denial of what was for Dōgen the basis for his own achievement—the conviction that all beings *just as they are* are Buddhas.

The second phrase highlighting the uniqueness of Dōgen's Zen is *shūshō ittō*, which means "the oneness of practice and enlightenment." *Shūshō ittō* points the way to correct practice by cautioning us not to think of enlightenment as a future event that will result from present practice. Instead, practicing *shūshō ittō*, we proceed in the knowledge that we are already that which we hope to become, and that our practice is the manifestation of this inherent enlightenment. Actually, it is not even we as sentient beings who engage in practice, it is the Buddha who practices. Consequently, there is no sequence of ignorance followed by enlightenment. When we practice Zen, we are Buddhas. Practice and enlightenment are the same; to practice is to be a Buddha.

When Dōgen returned to Japan after his trip to China, the first thing he wrote was *Fukan zazengi* ("General Recommendations for Doing Zazen"), and in it he said, "Do not sit [i.e., do zazen] in order to become a Buddha, because that has nothing to do with such things as sitting or lying down." We recall the famous dialogue between Master Huai-jang and Ma-tsu. Huai-jang found Ma-tsu doing zazen, and when asked why he was doing it, Ma-tsu replied, "To become a Buddha." Thereupon, Huai-jang sat down and began to polish a piece of brick. "Why are you polishing that brick?" asked Ma-tsu. "I'm going to turn it into a mirror," was the master's answer. "But," said Ma-tsu, "no amount of polishing will turn that brick into a mirror." "That is true," replied Huai-jang, "and no amount of zazen will turn you into a Buddha." This story is not meant to deny the necessity of practice—practice is essential; it is the heart of Buddhism and the key to learning the Way—but it is not a means to an end. True practice is the enlightened activity of the Buddha we already are.

Dōgen's understanding of practice turns the older, traditional Buddhist sequence of morality, meditation, and enlightenment (Skt. *shīla, samādhi, prajñā*) upside-down. In the Buddhism prior to Dōgen's time, a proper observance of moral and ethical injunctions was emphasized as the necessary, preliminary basis for the central practice of meditation. The rationale for this apparently is the obvious one: a person who is careless in his interpersonal relationships is just not the kind of person who can meditate effectively. Thus, the order of morality preceding meditation seems ultimately to have had a practical basis; and then in turn meditation leads to insight and enlightenment. However, Dōgen places enlightenment first, as the basis of both meditation and ethics, which themselves are in turn manifestations of enlightenment. Dōgen's views on the matter of ethics and morality led him to the conclusion that the real, practical observance of the precepts had to be an organic unfolding of a mode of conduct that was itself an expression of an enlightened nature. In fact, Dōgen says that ethics and meditation are the same thing: "When one does zazen, what ethical precepts are not being observed?" he asks. Both ethics and meditation are thus "wonderful practice based on intrinsic enlightenment." This is the life of a Buddha.

The idea that meditation, ethics, and enlightenment are all the same thing was not exactly Dōgen's innovation. The story about Huai-jang polishing a brick indicates that Dōgen's Chinese predecessors had already understood this relationship. The doctrine of "intrinsic enlightenment" is in fact one of the most obvious characteristics of Chinese Buddhism. This doctrine of intrinsic enlightenment is, in Dōgen's teaching, raised up to the status of the central and crucial fact, and it explains his whole approach to training in the Dharma. For Dōgen, it is not even really correct to say that it is the ordinary human being who is performing the practice; it is the Buddha who instigates the practice and maintains it. "No ordinary being ever became a Buddha," he says in *Yuibutsu yobutsu,* "only Buddhas become Buddhas."

Historically, the first clear statement of this insight occurs in the *Platform Sutra* of Hui-neng, the sixth ancestor of Chinese Zen. It is clear that there is continuity between Hui-neng's Zen and Dōgen's Zen. In the *Platform Sutra* Hui-neng says,

Good friends, my teaching of the Dharma takes meditation and wisdom as its basis. Never under any circumstances mistakenly say that meditation and wisdom are different; they are a unity, not two things. Meditation itself is the substance of wisdom; wisdom itself is the function of meditation. At the very moment when there is wisdom, then meditation exists in wisdom; at the very moment when there is meditation, then wisdom exists in meditation. Good friends, this means that meditation and wisdom are alike. Students, be careful not to say that meditation gives rise to wisdom, or that wisdom gives rise to meditation, or that meditation and wisdom are different from each other. To hold this view implies that things have duality.[1]

Hui-neng says clearly that what seem to be two things are in fact one. For Dōgen, too, wisdom and meditation are identical, and thus the duality of means and ends is overcome and the way to correct practice is shown. To sit upright with straight back, with mind and body unified, empty and unattached to internal and external events—this is itself Buddha wisdom; this is Buddha mind.

"Buddha-Tathāgatas," says Dōgen, "all have a wonderful means, which is unexcelled and free from human agency, for transmitting the wondrous Dharma from one to another without alteration and realizing supreme and complete awakening. That it is only transmitted without deviation from Buddha to Buddha is due to the *jijuyū samādhi*, which is its touchstone."[2] *Jijuyū samādhi* is another important term. It is in a way synonymous with zazen. *Ji* means "self" or "oneself," and *ju* and *yū* mean "receive" and "use," respectively. The samādhi called *jijuyū*, therefore, is meditation that one enjoys and uses oneself. It is contrasted with *tajuyū samādhi,* which is samādhi performed for some other purpose, such as for other beings or in order to acquire Buddhahood. Dōgen teaches that, rather than do zazen for some purpose, one sits quietly, without expectation, in jijuyū samādhi, simply to enjoy one's own inherent nature, without question of means and ends. This zazen practice is, according to Dōgen's *Fukan zazengi,* zazen in which we "gauge our enlightenment to the fullest."

According to Dōgen, Shakyamuni himself first enjoyed this samādhi while sitting under the bodhi tree for several days after his own realization. There was no question of using the samādhi for some ulterior purpose, because he had already obtained everything there was to obtain. Then why did he continue to sit in jijuyū samādhi? Because he was just manifesting and enjoying his Buddhahood. Yet eventually he rose and went on to teach his Dharma for the next forty-five years, for ultimately jijuyū samādhi is not separate from tajuyū samādhi; samādhi used for the benefit of others is not separate from samādhi enjoyed oneself. Sentient beings are numberless, and Buddhist practitioners, if they truly follow the Mahayana Way, must arouse the determination to do whatever they can to emancipate all these sentient beings by leading them to the other shore, to enlightenment.

Again we come to the following question: If one is in fact a Buddha right now, why practice at all? Isn't it enough that we are told by scripture and the personal testimony of masters that we are, always have been, and always will be Buddhas? This question plagued Dōgen in his younger years and eventually led him to China in search of answer. The answer itself is not really difficult to find, but it is vitally important that we understand it. We may know that we are Buddhas, but for most of us, this is not real knowledge. It is only hearsay, something we are told and that we may (or may not) accept on faith. However, our unrealized Buddha nature does not illuminate and transform our everyday lives. It is somewhat like having talent for music. We may be told we have this talent, and the knowledge may be gratifying, but we are still unable, for instance, to play the piano. The potential is real, but remains unactivated and unrealized. If the individual begins to practice, the talent itself will become evident in the practice. The ability to play the piano is a latent talent now realized. But if a talented person does not begin to practice, he might as well not have the ability. Our Buddha nature is like this. Dōgen tells us, "To disport oneself freely in this [jijuyū] samādhi, the right entrance is proper sitting in zazen. This Dharma is amply present in every person, but unless one practices, it is not manifested, unless there is realization, it is not attained."[3]

Dōgen Zenji himself speaks often of realization. The Japanese word that is translated as "realization" literally means "proof," "evidence," "certification," and "witnessing." All these words carry the sense of authenticating and bringing out into the open. The English word "realization" literally means "making real," which is close to the meaning of the Japanese term. Thus, realization of Buddha nature means making real for ourselves what otherwise is only hearsay. Buddhism is an experiential religion in which this real-making process actualizes Buddha nature as a concrete, lived reality.

Therefore, because practice is absolutely necessary for making our inherent Buddha nature a lived reality, practice never ends. As long as we imagine that practice is only a means to a greater end, we tend to think that once we have acquired some small insight, we no longer need to practice. But if in fact we are each a perfect and complete Buddha, then there can never be an end to the realization of this nature, for there is no limit to its ability to encompass more and more of experience. Indeed, a person who desires enlightenment ardently may for that reason be unable to acquire it, since by definition enlightenment is essentially desireless. In fact, Dōgen says that all that is required is simple faith in one's intrinsic Buddha nature,[4] and elsewhere, in *Shōji* ("Birth and Death") he says:

> You only attain the mind of Buddha when there is no hating and no desiring. But do not try to gauge it with your mind or speak it with words. When you simply release and forget both your body and mind and throw yourself into the house of Buddha, and when functioning comes from the direction of Buddha and you go in accord with it, then with no strength needed and no thought expended, freed from birth and death, you become Buddha. Then there can be no obstacle in any man's mind. There is an extremely easy way to become Buddha. Refraining from all evils, not clinging to birth and death, working in deep compassion for all sentient beings, respecting those over you and pitying those below you, without any detesting or desiring, worrying or lamentation— this is what is called Buddha. Do not search beyond it.[5]

This faith in one's intrinsic Buddha nature is the life of endless practice. To "throw ourselves into the house of the Buddha" is to have deep faith in the reality of this nature, and practice is simply allowing this nature to actualize or realize itself in our daily lives. It is practice forever. From time to time there may be flashes of *satori* insight, sometimes grand and overwhelming, sometimes small and modest, but practice goes on and on. The master may test the depth of our insight from time to time by means of judiciously chosen *kōans,* and may certify our understanding, but the practice continues. "When Buddhas are truly Buddhas," says Dōgen, "there is no need to know that we are all Buddhas, but we are realized Buddhas and further advance in realizing Buddha."[6] If, like Methuselah in the Hebrew scriptures, we were able to live for 900 years, we would continue to practice and continue to realize the Buddha. The horizons of Buddha vision are boundless and limitless, and the depths to which it can penetrate are fathomless.

This practice is very simple, but also very difficult. It is our human nature to pick and choose, to desire and loathe, to form myriad attitudes and judgments toward the events of our lives. This practice is difficult because it demands of us that we simply cease the picking and choosing, desiring and loathing. A contemporary Zen master has said that "Zen is picking up your coat from the floor and hanging it up." Nothing could be simpler. Yet how difficult! There is no fun in "picking up your coat." Tasks like this do not seem at all self-fulfilling and enriching. Even worse, "picking up your coat" doesn't seem to be a very "spiritual" kind of practice—unlike, we imagine, prayer, meditation, fasting, or developing a meaningful relationship. There is nothing more ordinary and unspecial than "picking up your coat." Yet, it is really the essence of practice, for "picking up your coat" is exactly what Dōgen means by meditation.

Just how is "picking up your coat" the essence of practice? It is particularly important for Western people to understand this, because we have all been raised in a culture where it is usually assumed that religious activities are of a special nature; indeed, that religion is a sphere separate from the mundane world. From this perspective, the statement that religious practice—meditation—consists of "picking up your coat" may seem absurd. We almost always pick up the coat, or wash the dishes, or perform any other task of that sort with regret or dislike, yearning to be elsewhere doing better things. We are bored, impatient, and perhaps even somewhat resentful. Doing things in this manner—our minds filled with likes and dislikes—is not Zen. But the rest of our lives will be made up of countless situations of this kind. Will we continue to approach them with irritation and regret, hoping for better things elsewhere, later, or will we begin to see this ordinary life as Buddha sees it? Possibly our ordinary life can in time come to seem good enough, even beautiful, to us, if we begin to practice meditation in Dōgen's way.

Unfortunately, most choose not to practice. Non-practice means continuing to approach every situation with self-centered attitudes. "Is it going to benefit me?" we ask, or "Is it a threat to me?" All about us we see things that we imagine are "good" or "bad," but these goods and bads are only good and bad *for me.* Our hierarchy of self-oriented values often becomes more complex and deep-rooted the older we become, and it is just this mesh of attitudes and valuations that obscures our Buddha nature. To realize our Buddha nature, we need to remove this mesh and come to see that dishwashing is not inherently "bad" and becoming, say, chairman of the board of directors is not inherently "good," for the good and bad we constantly perceive about us are only reflections of our self-concern. Dōgen's zazen, the jijuyū samādhi, is a way to eliminate this obscuring veil, for by its very nature it is the experience of events without subjective judgments. But it is not a preparation for the sake of a future realization; in jijuyū samādhi we begin to realize ourselves as Buddha right here and now. As we live this samādhi, we live the life of Buddha.

Ideally, this samādhi comes to be our everyday consciousness, wherever we are, at all times. It is not a special consciousness reserved for an hour in the meditation room in the morning and evening. Nor does it mean going about in a dreamy, semi-wakeful state, as if we were anesthetized or drugged. In samādhi we know pain as pain and pleasure as pleasure; the alert and receptive mind reflects all events clearly and without distortion. The only difference between samādhi and our ordinary self-consciousness is that in samādhi we do not correlate our experiences with some idea or judgment such as "good" or "bad." We live an experience one-hundred percent, without adding any subjective judgment to it.

Hui-neng defines this zazen practice in the following way:

What is it in this teaching we call sitting in meditation? In this teaching, sitting means without any obstruction anywhere, outwardly and under all circumstances, not to activate thoughts. Meditation is internally to see the original nature and not become confused.[7]

To sit, then, means to stop correlating external events with ideas such as "it is this," or "it is that," "right," "wrong," and so on, endlessly. Sitting has nothing to do with anesthesia or with escaping anything, for when the snow falls, we will still shiver and get our hair wet; when the pangs of disease strike, we will suffer the pain; and when the voracious tiger of old age springs, we will be devoured like everyone else. Dōgen says that the secret is not to hate these things nor desire their alternatives, but to to realize that these things— exactly as they are—are all there is. When the great Chinese Zen master Ta-mei was dying, his students asked him for a final helpful word. "When it comes, don't try to avoid it; when it goes, don't run after it," he said. Just then, a squirrel chattered on the roof. "There is only this, there is nothing else," said Ta-mei, and then he died. Can we conceive of what *this* is? Can *this* be enough for us? Is there another reality more real or more wonderful than *this*? To know that there is only *this* is to "see the original nature and not become confused."

The key to practice is the development of jijuyū samādhi and its expression as tajuyū samādhi in all activities. Daily formal sitting in zazen will establish a model for this samādhi that we can in time learn to retain and use to illuminate our ordinary life. When we "pick up the coat" as a Buddha activity, two things occur. First, it is no longer a profane or lowly act, but the very functioning of Buddha nature. Second, this and every act become ceaseless training through which this Buddha activity grows to include more and more within its scope. Because there are no limits to the amount of experience that can be illuminated by this activity, there is also no end to practice.

The practice I have been discussing might also be called the practice of the art of doing just one thing at a time. It is wonderful to learn to do one thing at a time. When we do formal zazen, we just sit; this means we do not add to the sitting any judgments such as how wonderful it is to do zazen, or how badly we are doing at it. We just sit. When we wash the dishes, we just wash dishes; when we drive on the highway, we just drive. When pain comes, there is just pain, and when pleasure comes, there is just pleasure. A Buddha is someone who it totally at one with his experience at every moment.

This practice is simple, but difficult. And the difficulty lies in not adding something extra to the events of our life.

In practicing Dōgen's Zen, there is really no big graduation day when the training stops, because we are already that which we seek, and practice is learning day-by-day to be what we are. The starting point is intrinsic Buddhahood. Real meditation is the alert, clear-minded attention to the details of daily life that emerges when we "do not activate thoughts." To attain this even to some slight extent is to realize one's Buddha nature to that extent. To realize this nature fully requires one to practice forever. This is what it means to follow Dōgen's Way.

Practice must therefore include all activities; it cannot be limited to the formal activities of the zendō, when we chant, bow, offer incense, and do zazen. Zazen must begin when we open our eyes in the morning and not even end when we close them at night, so that all the activities of the day become practice. Sometimes many or most of these other activities do not feel like practice. Earning money to eat, maintaining the buildings and grounds in which we practice and live, keeping our living quarters neat and clean, treating food and clothing with respect and gratitude, following the many regulations of any community of people—these are often thought of as distractions from real practice, nuisances, or at best necessary concessions that support real practice. Dōgen reminds us that it is not hard to desire to practice, to seek out a teacher, and to enter the activities of the meditation hall, but harder to do all the other things that we do not associate with practice. "Entering the deep mountains and thinking about the Buddha Way is comparatively easy, while building stupas and making Buddha images is very difficult," he says. These things are difficult because unless a person has a very real commitment to following the Way and understands this commitment as a total response to all events and all activities, ordinary activities feel like a burden.

All our activities are ideally gestures of respect toward the Buddha, the Dharma, and the Sangha. Learning the Way must therefore include niceties of etiquette between individuals who practice together, for this is nothing nmore than respect for their Buddha nature.

Many things that need to be done are not for ourselves but for our successors, like Lin-chi planting cedars for those who would come after him. The Mahayana emphasis on helping all living beings thus includes not only those living now but also those who will come after us. All these activities become practice for the person who has what Dōgen called "the mind that seeks the Way." When one has dropped off mind and body and no longer hankers for fame and profit, when one lives one's life just as do the birds that sing in the trees, when one is truly grateful to the Buddha and his descendents, then all activities become practice. When there is no distinction of sacred and profane, profitable and nonprofitable, practice and nonpractice, then every gesture is practice in learning the Way. This is learning to raise an ox.

The most impressive aspect of Dōgen's Way is the insistence on utter seriousness and utter commitment. It is inspiring to read any of the writings of Dōgen, for he tolerates no half-hearted, self-serving, or dilettantish involvement in the Way. One must pursue the Way in the single-minded and earnest manner of a person trying to extinguish a fire in his hair. Anything less than this is only a waste of our time, for we will never succeed unless learning the Way is the most important thing in our lives. How can anyone hope to measure up to Dōgen's demanding requirements? Practice exacts our full effort at all times. To read the various chapters on practice in the *Shōbōgenzō* is to become aware of what a rare person Dōgen was, and why there is no grander conception of the religious life to be found anywhere.

The ten chapters I have translated are all about this ceaseless practice, though philosophy is not entirely absent. I have chosen these ten chapters for several reasons. They represent the various dimensions of practice, they are powerful and beautiful in their spirit and rhetorical force, they exhibit so well Dōgen's stern and uncompromising spirit, and they are among the most moving I have encountered. There are surely other chapters of *Shōbōgenzō* that could have been included. For instance, any collection ought to include *Genjō kōan*, which is pertinent to practice and is surely one of the most brilliant, profound, and moving religious documents in world religious literature. I have not included it because it has already been well translated by others, and I cannot improve on these translations.[8]

Also, I might have included a chapter on atonement, which, perhaps surprisingly, is very important in Dōgen's ideas about practice.

The following expository chapters are included here in the earnest hope that they will help to clarify just what Dōgen Zenji means by practice, although just what the essence of that practice is, is beyond my powers to express. Dōgen uses several expressions to indicate the same thing. For example, we might say that the essence of practice is *shinjin datsuraku,* which means "mind and body dropped off." It is synonymous with "emptiness," and denotes a state in which one is no longer motivated by self-concern. But it seems clear from the essays translated here that, in a very real way, *shinjin datsuraku* is the same as *shukke,* which means "home departure." Consequently, to really leave home, or the world, is the same as dropping off mind and body. However, again, both terms can be seen as identical with *hotsu mujō shin,* "arousing the supreme thought," or "arousing the determination to attain the supreme." Continuous practice *(gyōji)* is none other than the whole of daily activity performed by one who embodies these things. If we grasp such interconnections among Dōgen's terms, we will find the essence of practice is enunciated clearly in all the chapters of *Shōbōgenzo* translated here. They allow us to obtain some idea of what it is that Dōgen's Way requires.

Essays

The Importance of Faith

Practice is not possible without faith. It may be startling to hear that faith is important in Zen, but the fact is that it has always been an important part of Buddhism throughout its twenty-five-hundred-year history. Prior to the experiential realization of the truth of the Buddha's teachings, one must proceed with practice in the faith that the teachings are true and that through practice we will realize our Buddha nature. Without this faith, there is no support for the practice, and if there is doubt or lack of assurance, one will either not begin practice or will not continue it through one's inevitable difficulties. In all of Buddhism prior to the arising of the Zen tradition, faith has thus had a crucial function in the life of the meditator. Many of the lists of practices, mental states, and stages of development of the early abhidharma literature include *shraddha* (faith). When meditators begin to verify the teachings of Buddha in their own experience, faith is superceded by direct knowledge. This differs from the Christian tradition, for instance, where faith remains the central way of religious expression throughout the life of the "believer." For Christians, there is never a time when faith is no longer important, for the tenets of their belief are not experientially validated in the same way as the doctrines of Buddhism. For Buddhists, faith, while it is necessary in the first phase of development, is something that eventually becomes transformed. In Buddhism there is a vast difference between *believing* that all things are impermanent and *realizing* that they are; but before that belief becomes true knowledge, one must practice in the faith that it is so, and will eventually be proven to be so by one's own experience.

Before going on, it might be well to define Buddhist faith. We can begin by examining the kinds of faith. First of all, faith may be the intellectual acceptance of a doctrine or creed. In this case, faith amounts to an act of the will, whereby the individual feels that he *ought* to accept such-and-such a teaching and thus does so. I may be taught that a supernatural being exists, and in order to qualify as an orthodox member of a community, I will agree, even though there is no basis in my own experience for doing so. In fact, many people profess belief in a god, in resurrection of the body, and in final judgment, but their merely intellectual acceptance of these ideas is evident from the fact that their lives do not correspond to their belief. Second, faith may take the form of passionate commitment to an idea that can never really be validated experientially. For instance, I will never in this life know (in the strict sense) if personal immortality is a fact, but I may choose nonetheless to cling tenaciously to the idea and organize my life in accordance with it. Third, faith may approach a kind of certainty, because the object of faith is a common, recurrent phenomenon in one's life and therefore seems to merit faith: I can have faith in the rising of the sun tomorrow morning because it has risen every morning of my life so far. Though there is always a chance that it may not rise tomorrow morning, I can be reasonably justified in my faith. This is an easy kind of faith because I can rely on past experience.

But none of the above examples closely resembles Buddhist faith. Buddhist faith is a deep certitude as to the veracity of a certain doctrine, accepted and used as a touchstone for conduct in confidence that one's practice will verify its truth. The object of faith may be an idea, one's teacher, or the trustworthiness of the Buddha himself, but in any case, there is a complete certainty that one is encountering something on which one may totally rely. The object of faith may be trusted provisionally because Buddhism itself teaches that the faith will eventually be replaced by knowledge and that any teaching not verifiable in this way ought to be rejected. Consequently, Buddhist faith is not blind and irrational, nor is it a mere intellectual adherence to creedal orthodoxy. Acceptance of Buddhist doctrines is provisional because of the necessity of eventually replacing faith in them with experiential knowledge. Thus faith is anticipation of validation. This faith is further strengthened because of one's association with people who actualize their own experiential knowledge in their lives. And because Zen Buddhism as a religion is based on each individual's realization of the Buddha's own enlightenment, ideally, there can never be a question of reliance on faith alone throughout life.

The various chapters of *Shōbōgenzō* show that there can be several objects of faith, but in the final analysis, all are the same. One has faith in the Buddha, and one must have faith in one's teacher— one's teacher is a kind of surrogate Buddha inasmuch as he has inherited the Buddha's mind from his own teacher, and so on, back to the time of Shakyamuni himself. This is the meaning of the ancestral succession in the lineage of teachers. One must also have faith in the teachings of Buddhism—but are these not merely verbal expressions of the Buddha mind? And one must have faith in one's own intrinsic Buddha nature. This faith is the very door through which one enters the Dharma. Dōgen therefore remarks, "The Buddha once said, 'The person who is without faith is like a broken jug.' This means that living beings who do not have faith in the Buddha's teaching cannot be vessels of the teaching. The Buddha also said, 'The great ocean of the Buddha's teaching is entered through the door of faith.' Clearly know that those beings who have no faith are those people who do not dwell in it."[9]

Thus, faith is the entryway to the Dharma. Correct practice is based on the faith that one is already a Buddha, for there is nothing that is not the Buddha. "Grass, trees, all are [One] mind and body," says Dōgen in *Hotsu mujō shin*. "If the myriad dharmas are not born, neither is the One Mind born. If all dharmas are marked with this ultimate reality, then [even] a speck of dust is marked with it. The One Mind is all dharmas; all dharmas are the One Mind, the whole body."[10] Consequently, unless practice is undertaken in the faith that oneself is the Buddha, and that everything else, even a speck of dust, is also the Buddha and preaches the Dharma with a clear voice, realization of the fact will be impossible.

Dōgen did not compose a separate chapter on faith in *Shōbōgenzō,* but there are many scattered statements about it in various chapters in the *Shōbōgenzō* and elsewhere that leave no doubt that it is the basis for the practice of Dōgen's Way. For instance, in *Gakudō yōjinshū* (which is not part of *Shōbōgenzō*), he says,

> Practicing the Way of the Buddha means you must have faith in the Buddha Way. Having faith in the Buddha Way means you first must have faith that you originally abide in the Way, are not deluded, are not mistaken, neither gain nor lose [in Buddha wisdom] and are not in error. If you arouse this kind of faith, illuminate the Way in this manner, and rely on it and practice it, it is the basis for enlightenment.[11]

Faith is not only the basis for practice and the entry into the Dharma, it is practice itself.

Zazen, for instance, is surely the main practice in Dōgen's Zen, but practice takes other forms also, as I have already indicated in the first chapter. Home departure *(shukke)* is practice, as is receiving and maintaining the precepts *(jukai)*, venerating all the Buddhas, taking the threefold refuge *(kie sambō)*, wearing the robes of a monk, repenting one's past bad deeds *(karma)*, making images and reliquary containers (stupas), asking questions of the master, and still other things as well. It is interesting that Dōgen interprets all these forms of practice as expressions of faith. Atonement, for example, which Dōgen says is the examination of one's own wicked behavior, is not just a verbal confession and a decision not to do evil again, but in essence consists of a reaffirming of faith and rededication to practice. To have faith in the Buddha and his teaching and to commit oneself to hard practice without reservation is atonement.[12] Taking refuge in the Three Treasures means relying completely on Buddha, Dharma, and Sangha, and not on one's own abilities, so that taking refuge in them is itself a statement of faith in their reality and power. In *Kie sambō* ("Taking Refuge in the Three Treasures"), Dōgen says,

> With regard to taking refuge in the Three Treasures, with pure faith in your abdomen, whether the Tathāgata dwells in the world or does not, join the palms of your hands together, bow your

head, and say, "I, from now on until I become a Buddha, take refuge in the Buddha, I take refuge in his teaching, I take refuge in the community of followers."[13]

Dōgen's attitude toward the monk's robe *(kesa)* is also instructive. The kesa is not just clothing worn by a specific group of people to distinguish them from others; it is to be treated with great respect because it symbolizes and embodies the Dharma itself. Thus, to take the precepts and wear the kesa is to acknowledge faith in the Dharma and to wear the Dharma on one's body. Dōgen tells us,

It is clear that the Dharma that is symbolized by the kesa has been transmitted from master to master. To think that it is without value or that it has not been correctly transmitted is evidence of lack of faith. He who is interested in arousing the thought of enlightenment must be instructed in the correct transmission of the ancestors. He is then not only a person who has encountered the Dharma, which is hard to encounter, he is in fact a descendent of the Dharma that is correctly transmitted in the form of the Buddha's robe. He sees it, learns it, and now wears the robe. In other words, he is in reality standing right in front of the Buddha, meeting him, hearing him preach the Dharma, and being illuminated by his light. [Wearing the kesa] means using what the Buddha used and transmitting the Buddha's mind to oneself. It means acquiring the essence of the Buddha.[14]

The object of faith in this passage is twofold: Dharma itself as taught by the Buddha, and the Zen master as one who has inherited this Dharma in the ancestral succession. The kesa that one wears is the visible Dharma, and wearing it expresses one's faith.

The merits of the kesa enable us to realize the truth within ourselves: "The kesa correctly transmits the skin, flesh, bones, and marrow of Shakyamuni, the Blessed One.... Those who receive the kesa, wear it, and hold it reverently to their heads will without doubt become enlightened."[15] Thus to put on the kesa is putting on the Dharma, as the "Verse of the Kesa" says:

How wonderful is the robe of liberation,
A markless field of merit.
I place the Buddha's teaching on my body,
And liberate living beings everywhere.[16]

Such passages serve to show that faith is the indispensable basis for practice. In *Bendōwa,* Dōgen says,

> The realm of Buddhas is inconceivable and beyond the reach of the intellect. How can it be reached by someone who has no faith, who has little knowledge? Only a person with a great motive can attain it. For the person who is lacking in faith, it is impossible. When right faith arises in the mind, one should practice and study under a master.[17]

Certainly, faith is important, but the truth of the matter can be expressed in an even stronger way: Dōgen's Zen is the Zen of faith. That is, it is a religion in which faith is the very mechanism whereby the goal is achieved, and in the absence of which the door to the truth remains closed. It is therefore not simply one important element among others; it is the indispensable prerequisite.

Japanese and Chinese Buddhists have for centuries distinguished the various forms of Buddhism by means of a system called (in Japanese) *kyōhan,* "doctrinal classification." In this system, a dominant characteristic of each form of Buddhism is isolated and used to distinguish between that form and all other forms. For example, the Pure Land Buddhism of Shinran has always referred to itself as the "way of faith," while all other forms, including Zen, are referred to as the "saintly way." The "saintly way" refers to practices that presumably involve meditation, concern with moral purification, learning, and the like. It has also been said that Pure Land Buddhism is the way of "other power," while Zen and other forms of Buddhism are the way of "self power." The reason for this is that in Pure Land Buddhism, the way is through complete dependence on the saving power of another, specifically the Buddha Amida, while Zen practitioners depend on their own efforts to achieve emancipation. Faith is important in a different way in Pure Land Buddhism than it is in Dōgen's Zen.[18]

One way to make sense of the bewildering proliferation of Buddhist schools, doctrines, and practices over the last 2,500 years is to see them as a single, creative, ongoing effort to deal with the central problem of samsaric existence, which is the erroneous belief in an enduring, permanent self. Whether it is Zen, Pure Land, Theravada, or Tibetan Buddhist practice, all Buddhist paths teach practices that will effectively destroy the belief in this self. Dōgen's Zen, with its stress on faith, is no different; that is, the mechanism of faith is effective in dealing with the problem of the self. The necessity of *shinjin datsuraku,* the "dropping off of body and mind," is the necessity of understanding that oneself, and all other beings, are empty of this self that is only a convenient fiction.

How does one drop off body and mind? How does one achieve emptiness? It seems that there have been primarily two different ways of achieving this result in the history of world Buddhism. The way of pre-Mahayana Buddhism and the Theravada Buddhism of present-day Southeast Asia and Sri Lanka has been the way of frontal assault. This is the method of *shamatha* and *vipassanā* meditations, which first put obstructive emotions and impulses to sleep in *shamatha* exercises, then subject the self to the corrosive analysis of *vipassanā* insight practices. The final achievement is the destruction of the illusory self. The other method, which is generally Mahayana and takes various forms, is an indirect method. It is indirect because instead of attacking the idea of a self directly, the illusion is destroyed in the process of directing one's will and attention away from the self. The Mahayana emphasis on compassion and the bodhisattva's career of selfless service on behalf of others gradually diminishes self-serving, self-interested action. The saying "to help others is to help oneself" means that in the process of devoting oneself unconditionally to helping all living beings, one becomes more and more capable of acting in a non-selfserving manner. I would like to suggest that faith accomplishes the same goal in Dōgen's Zen. And, of course, because this Zen is Mahayana Buddhism, there is the same bodhisattva vow, so that the individual involved in this Zen practice is working toward the goal in the traditional Mahayana fashion. The approach must be indirect, in a way, because the direct pursuit of enlightenment is a confession of dualistic thinking and merely one more attempt to seek ego-gratification.

This is why Dōgen Zenji so often warns against any kind of seeking or wanting, even if the object of the desire is a "holy" object or enlightenment itself. "If you wish to practice the Way of the Buddhas and ancestors, you should follow without thought of profit the Way of the former sages and the conduct of the ancestors, expecting nothing, seeking nothing, and gaining nothing. Cut off the mind that seeks and do not cherish a desire to gain the fruits of Buddhahood," he says in the *Zuimonki*.[19] But how does one practice if one should not think of practicing *for* something?

There are several ways of doing this in Mahayana Buddhism. One method, about which I will speak in detail in the next chapter, is that of making a vow to emancipate all living beings even though oneself is not completely emancipated; this is the traditional bodhisattva vow. By practicing in this manner, even though one has an objective (to emancipate all living beings), it is not a self-gratifying objective. The other method is to commit oneself utterly to practicing the Way, but in the understanding that it is not merely oneself who is carrying out the practice: Thus, when one sits in zazen, it is not the individual self who sits, but the Buddha who sits, and thus all beings. The gradual clarification of one's experience as a result of zazen is not the result of the individual clarifying and spiritualizing his own mind, but the result of the Buddha being a Buddha; that is, it is the Buddha who is realizing Buddhahood, as Dōgen says. And this begins to happen when we completely abandon our own efforts and trust completely in our true nature, which is the Buddha. Again, this is Buddhist faith.

Faith is important in Dōgen's Zen because practice must be undertaken in trust in another—the Buddha. This is the necessary basis of practice. Seen in this way, Dōgen's Zen is not really the Buddhism of self power *(jiriki)*, it is the Buddhism of other power *(tariki)*. One may indeed practice the Buddhism of self power, and many do, but it will not be Dōgen's way. Dōgen's approach to practice and realization is the culmination of Buddhism's historical attempt to deal with the problem of the self and its actions, and is thus a most sophisticated and profound solution to the problem.

In Shinran's Pure Land Buddhism, it is taught that liberation and final nirvana are gifts given by Amida and not states attained by our own efforts. Moreover, in order for Amida's wonderful gifts to become a reality for us, we must *not* try to gain them by our own efforts. In a time countless cosmic eons in the past, when Amida was still a practicing bodhisattva named Dharmākara, he made a number of vows, the essence of which was that he, Dharmākara, would never enter into the state of final, complete Buddhahood until and unless every other living being also achieved the same Buddhahood. Through countless, inconceivable practices he accumulated a vast store of merit and finally did become the Buddha Amida. What this means is that in some sense, all living beings are guaranteed Buddhahood, and therefore also, in some sense, are already Buddhas, because the condition of the vows was that Dharmākara would not become a Buddha unless every other living being did also. The fact of his present Buddhahood implies the present Buddhahood of all beings. In other words, the conditions of the vow are fulfilled. Once an individual becomes aware of what Amida has done for him, that is, once faith in the vows has arisen in his heart, he is then reborn in Amida's paradise when he dies, where he will speedily achieve enlightenment. The key to rebirth in the Western Paradise of Amida is unshakable faith in the vows.

When we look deeper into this matter of faith and try to determine what is actually happening in the life of the believer, it becomes evident that faith exactly coincides with the complete abandonment of self-effort and a turning to Amida, for as was pointed out above, self-effort is itself an admission of doubt in the power of Amida's vows. As D.T. Suzuki and others have noted, if we strip away the mythological trappings of the situation, we find that what is spoken of as a kind of knowledge that one has really been saved by Amida, is a form of satori, and this satori occurs when, and only when, the individual ceases to rely on his own power and ability. Is this not the forgetting of the self that Dōgen speaks of in *Genjō kōan?* Can there be a more powerful form of this self-forgetting than abandoning oneself completely to the Other?

Thus, the reason why faith is necessary, and is so powerful, is that in turning completely to the Other, we begin to forget the self and its incessant demands. It might be said that the human tendency to seek self-gratification through self-reliance begins to diminish in inverse ratio to our faith and trust in our inherent Buddha nature and its ability to actualize itself. Thus, Dōgen tells us to throw ourselves into the house of the Buddha. A young Sōtō Zen monk once remarked, "We can find complete freedom and tranquility in ourselves when we have left ourselves completely to the Buddha's boundlessly wide mind."[20] Dōgen knew this from his own experience, and therefore his life was spent teaching a Buddhism of faith in the power of the Other, who is the Buddha.

It is difficult to overstate the matter: To have faith in the Buddha is the same as forgetting the self. How can it be otherwise when the prime requirement for "learning the Way" is to forget the self, *shinjin datsuraku?* The dropping off of one's own body and mind and the minds and bodies of others is the almost incredible and inconceivable act of becoming totally empty, whereby we are no longer attached to anything (even nirvana), in which there is nothing to desire, nothing to expect, nothing to be. The vexing dualisms of life are transcended and all discriminations cease to operate. But how does one achieve this life if practice itself is a greater attachment, and if one's practice is based on dualisms even more absolute than the ordinary ones? It is like trying to fight fire with fire—an even greater entanglement in contradictions and confusion.

In the final analysis, there is really no difference between this faith and zazen itself. The definition of zazen in the first chapter was that *sitting* means not activating thoughts toward external events, and *Zen* means seeing one's true nature and not being confused. True zazen, then, is any activity carried out without self-concern, not forming self-serving attitudes toward events, and living one's ordinary life without attachment or loathing. This is the same as forgetting the self. To forget this self is to have faith in the ability of the Buddha to illuminate our lives with Buddha insight. Nothing more is required. Thus, Dōgen says:

> When I see an ignorant old monk sitting wordlessly, I think of the story of the woman with faith who became enlightened by giving a feast. It does not depend on knowledge, books, words, or long explanations. It just requires the aid of true faith.[21]

Arousing the Thought
of Enlightenment

IT IS EASY TO merely play the game in a formal discipline such as Zen. It is pleasant and rewarding to wear meditation robes, chant the sutras, bow to the Buddha, and sit in zazen. Anyone who has done much chanting knows that it gives one a feeling of euphoria, and one may think that this good feeling is spiritual or that it indicates growth. And nonetheless, activities such as chanting, bowing, and sitting in zazen are valuable, even when done merely in outward form, for even a superficial encounter with the Dharma will have some wholesome outcome at a later time. However, this is not true Zen. To follow the Dharma involves a complete reorientation of one's life in such a way that one's activities are filled with, and manifest, a deeper meaning. Otherwise, if merely sitting were enough, every frog in the pond would be enlightened, as one Zen master said. Dōgen himself said that one must practice Zen as if trying to "extinguish a fire in one's hair"—with an attitude of single-minded urgency.

True Zen therefore must be the dominant concern in one's life. One must cultivate a change in attitude toward all the "ordinary" activities in one's life. This is a reordering of values, really, because now, instead of seeking ultimate fulfillment and goodness in pleasure, power, wealth, or a fine reputation, one sees one's Dharma practice as having the greatest value and the greatest potential for fulfillment. As I will explain in a later chapter, this reorientation of values is also called "home departure" *(shukke),* but here I will discuss it in terms of a sincere, profound determination to follow the

Dharma. The traditional term for this is "arousing the thought of enlightenment" (Skt., *bodhicittotpāda;* Jap., *hotsu bodai shin*).

This new determination to follow the Dharma is not a simple matter of coolly deciding that one is going to start meditating and living a more "spiritual" life. Decisions of this sort are very easily rescinded, whereas a true decision to follow the Dharma cannot be. The determination to follow the Dharma is, on the one hand, a kind of conversion that is deep and moving, because it signals a profound disillusionment with life as it is lived by most people. It comes with the realization that real contentment and goodness do not come from sensual self-gratification, controlling the destinies of other people, or being what is conventionally considered an important, successful person. We recognize a fundamental hollowness, a basic unsatisfactoriness, in our present way of living. But, on the other hand, there is a realization—a faith—that the Dharma has the potential to restore clarity, sanity, contentment, and supreme goodness to our everyday, ordinary lives. To experience this disillusionment and to decide to follow the Dharma at all costs is what is meant by arousing the thought of enlightenment.

True determination to follow the Dharma at all costs may involve gladly sacrificing, if necessary, those things we have in the past held precious. Dōgen is fond of reminding us of the example of Hui-k'o, the second ancestor of Chinese Zen, who cut off his arm and offered it to Bodhidharma in order to convince him of his utmost sincerity and determination. This is a teaching that we must be prepared to offer even our lives in order to acquire the Dharma, because if anything is valued more than the Dharma, we have not yet aroused the thought of enlightenment, and without this determination, we cannot acquire the Dharma. The sixth ancestor, Hui-neng left his old and beloved mother in order to practice under Hung-jen, and Dōgen's own master, Ju-ching, did zazen even when his buttocks were covered with bloody sores from sitting in zazen. And there are many stories of Zen masters who suffered hunger and cold in order to practice Zen.

This new orientation in our lives, toward the Dharma, is truly a remarkable event, because it is a radical reordering of priorities. But it is remarkable also because it is the manifestation in our lives of a deeper and wiser mind. It is, in fact, the Buddha within us, awakening from slumber. Therefore, arousing the thought of enlightenment may also be said to be the arousing of the enlightened mind, for while on the one hand it is the new determination to realize our Buddha nature, it is also the awakening of this nature itself. This is why Dōgen praises the event so extravagantly: "This thought of enlightenment, this development of practice, transcends the bounds of enlightenment and delusion. It is superior to anything else in the universe, and is preeminent in all things."[22] This event is the determination of the Buddha to be realized through us; that is, it is a specific manifestation of the Dharmakaya, the cosmic Buddha body.

The prominence of the doctrine of arousing the thought of enlightenment in Dōgen's writings establishes him firmly within the Mahayana Buddhist tradition, but in the way he deepened its meaning, he arrived at what is doubtlessly the most sophisticated version of the idea in Buddhism. The idea of "arousing the thought of enlightenment" is as old as Mahayana Buddhism and is explained and extolled in almost all the major sutras and treatises of Mahayana literature. A typical treatment is to be found in Shantideva's *Bodhicāryāvatāra.*[23] In texts of this sort, the arousal of the thought of enlightenment marks the beginning of the bodhisattva's endless career of drawing closer and closer to complete, perfect enlightenment. It is an endless career because while in theory one will eventually attain this goal, in reality one will never attain it. The awakening of this determination to attain supreme enlightenment is accompanied by certain vows of a most serious nature, and this utter commitment starts the individual on the way through this life—and all lives—in search of the goal; but the search does not really begin until the thought of enlightenment has occurred. Without the commitment, there is no practice, and without practice, there is no attainment.

Why and how does this thought arise in the first place? What transforms an ordinary person into an utterly committed follower of the Way? The instinct to preserve, nourish, and enhance the self is so basic, so powerful, that it is almost impossible for most people to begin living life in any other way that is not a prolonged strategy for self-protection. Yet this is just what the bodhisattva does when he arouses the thought of enlightenment.

In Dōgen's writings, the thought of enlightenment is closely bound up with the perception of impermanence. To confront impermanence means to become radically aware of the transiency of one's own life and the other things that constitute our experience, such as friends, success, health, lovers, family, fame, pleasure, and even the great abstractions such as progress, honor, and the American way of life. Once we see that they cannot last and that we are completely incapable of hanging on to them, they cease to hold a grip on us. We finally realize that they are not fit objects of our concern. Our own lives slip away just as quickly and relentlessly as the other things we cherish, and not only can we not take our treasures with us when we depart, we cannot even take our bodies and minds. Thus, there is a tendency to ask just how we ought to spend the few precious days allotted to us. A well-known, old Buddhist verse says:

Alas, all conditioned things are impermanent;
It is their nature to come into being and then cease to be.
For having come into being, they will surely cease to be;
Their cessation is bliss.

For Dōgen, the perception of impermanence gives rise to a determination to seek the Dharma. It is probably accurate to say that throughout the history of Buddhism, the thought of enlightenment has been connected with the perception of impermanence; in Dōgen's thinking the connection seems to have grown out of his own experience. His first confrontation with impermanence occurred when, as a boy of seven, he sat watching the smoke of the incense disappear into the air at his mother's funeral. His father had died when he was only two years old, and five years later his beloved mother had died. The smoke of the incense fading into the air must have deeply impressed him with the impermanence and brevity of those things we long for and love. "This body, hair, and skin result from the union of the sperm and egg of the father and mother. If your heart stops, will not this body be scattered on mountains and fields and turn completely into mud? Really, where can one take hold of oneself?" he asks, in the *Zuimonki*.[24] Thus Dōgen turned to the Dharma at a very young age, determined to follow it, and eventually achieved a lasting place in the succession of great Zen masters. His own attainment was the result of an intensely seeking spirit, and this seeking spirit was the result of a deep perception of impermanence. In essay after essay of the *Shōbōgenzō,* he cautions us not to waste time in the face of this inexorable impermanence, but to make haste and enter the Way.

The perception of impermanence, then, is the motivation for entering the Way and making a supreme effort. In the first essay he wrote, *Fukan zazengi,* Dōgen took pains to emphasize the fact of impermanence in a work primarily devoted to the technique of zazen:

> Do not pass over from the light to the darkness by ignoring practice and pursuing other things. Take care of this essential instrument of the Buddha Way [which is your life]. Could you ever be content with the sparks from a stone [when the sun is blazing overhead]? That is not all; your body is like a dew-drop on the morning grass, your life is as brief as a flash of lightning. Momentary and vain, it is lost in a moment.[25]

Here, the practice of zazen is intimately connected with the fact of universal impermanence, for the urgency of practice is necessitated by impermanence.

An individual turns to the Dharma because it promises to remove the distress of life and bring about a deep reconciliation with this very impermanence. We undertake the practice of the Way because we have faith in the existence within ourselves of a potential for complete contentment, a contentment that is impossible to find in the pursuit of fame and profit. But it needs to be said over and over again, so as not to misconstrue the nature of Mahayana Buddhism, that this Way-seeking is not, in the end, simply another form of self-gratification. We hope, and expect, that following the Way will lead to a better understanding of ourselves and the rest of the world, and that we will achieve a degree of serenity and contentment. But, is any kind of progress in self-betterment truly possible as long as practice is undertaken with the primarily selfish desire to improve one's own lot? Is the goal of realization of one's Buddha nature compatible with a practice performed in the greedy expectation of one's own future happiness while blithely ignoring the unhappiness of the rest of the world? The Mahayana Buddhist answer to this question has always been no.

The Mahayana emphasis on compassion and the exaltation of the bodhisattva as the ideal individual are based on this understanding, that any goodness one personally derives from following the Dharma is a product of one's primary aspiration to help all other beings to achieve happiness in their lives. In other words, practice is undertaken in order to help others, and the bodhisattva's own slow progress toward final, complete enlightenment is the result of this other-directed activity. Thus to help others is to help oneself. It may also be said that to help oneself is to help others, since real, effective help is not possible as long as we ourselves are deluded and filled with greed and hatred. Therefore, the achievement of insight and understanding serves to make one capable of guiding and helping others. To wish to escape pain and trouble oneself and to ignore other creatures means that neither oneself nor others will find help. It is of the nature of things that we all progress together, and so we must seek the Dharma with this in mind.

Knowing, then, that a mean, selfish aspiration is not a real Buddhist aspiration, the bodhisattva begins his compassionate career with vows to emancipate all others, even before he himself is completely emancipated. The four bodhisattva vows, which are chanted daily in Zen training centers, are a public reminder of what the individual's training is all about:

> Sentient beings are innumerable; I vow to save them.
> Desires are inexhaustible; I vow to end them.
> The Dharma teachings are boundless; I vow to master them.
> The Buddha Way is unsurpassable; I vow to attain it.

The person who utters these vows in all sincerity is thus the Mahayana bodhisattva. It does not matter what color the robes of the monk are, what his ordination lineage is, or where he lives, for the Mahayana is a state of mind, and the bodhisattva is the person who makes these vows and means them. This vowing itself is the arousing of the thought of enlightenment. Dōgen makes this clear in *Hotsu bodai shin* when he says, "What is called arousing of the thought of enlightenment is the uttering of the vow to emancipate all living beings even while you yourself are not yet emancipated. When one arouses this thought, no matter how humble in appearance one is, one then becomes the guide of all beings."[26] If, as Dōgen says elsewhere, a Buddha is simply one whose main mission in the world is to guide all beings to the bliss of nirvana, then this vow must itself be the vow of the Buddha that we already are. Buddha *is* boundless compassion; who else can make such a loving, selfless vow?

The form of the vow indicates that the person who makes it will refuse the ultimate prize of complete enlightenment until and unless all other beings attain it first. Nor is this vow restricted only to human, or even sentient beings, but it includes trees, grass, shrubs, and stones as well. This is because Mahayana compassion and the bodhisattva's vow are not directed solely toward the human realm, for if it excluded nonhuman beings, it would not be perfect compassion, it would not be unconditional. The cycle of birth and death and its suffering includes all living things, not just human life. Now obviously the number of beings to be saved is indeed vast, even innumerable, as the vow says, and because bodhisattvas are really only human beings, and limited in the way all conditioned beings are, it would seem that in reality there will never be a time when their work is finished. Thus, in making the vow, they destine themselves to be forever excluded from the ultimate goal. In life after life, in all the realms of suffering, bodhisattvas work ceaselessly to save all others, while they themselves are never completely free of pain and delusion. One of the startling paradoxes of Mahayana Buddhism is that it is the bodhisattva alone—skillful, wise, and compassionate—who will never attain full, perfect Buddhahood, always remaining behind while others go on.

So what, after all, is a Buddha? What, after all, is perfect enlightenment? Buddhists over two thousand years ago asked these same questions, and in answering them created the movement within Buddhism that we now know as Mahayana. True enlightenment, they said, is not the complete, final cutting-off of the round of rebirth and suffering and the entering of final nirvana *(nirupadhi-*

shesa nirvana). Instead, one achieves the only real enlightenment precisely at that point when, out of compassion for the suffering of living beings, one deliberately refuses to attain the stage of final nirvana and enlightenment unless all other living beings attain it too. Thus, the paradox is that in refusing what is traditionally considered to be the ultimate goal of Buddhism and choosing to remain behind to serve as a guide, one really acquires the only true enlightenment and nirvana.[27]

It cannot really be otherwise. If enlightenment is, among other things, complete selflessness, then only when we have rid ourselves of selfishness to the point where we are no longer greedy even for the fruits of training do we really reach the "goal" of the Way. In gladly giving up the goal, we acquire it. The arousing of the thought of enlightenment, then, which Dōgen says is the compassionate vow to save all beings, is really a remarkable, wonderful occasion. It is remarkable and wonderful because the very ability to make such a vow and mean it most sincerely must be the appearance in one's life of a selflessness and compassion that are truly Buddha-like. It is, according to Dōgen Zenji, the manifesting of Buddha nature itself.

Dōgen says in *Hotsu bodai shin,*

> In Buddhism, the ultimate attainment is *bodhi,* which is also Buddhahood. If the highest, perfect enlightenment *(anuttara samyak sambodhi)* is compared with the initial arousing of the thought of enlightenment, it is like comparing the great conflagration at the time of the world's end with the light of a firefly. Still, if one arouses the thought of enlightenment, the thought of emancipating all other living beings even before one is emancipated oneself, there is no difference between the two. A Buddha is simply a person who thinks, "How can I cause beings to enter the supreme Dharma and rapidly become Buddhas?" This is the life of a Tathāgata.[28]

However, even this exertion of one's own inherent enlightenment nature in the perpetual act of helping all others to realize their enlightenment nature is not the final truth. After all, Shakyamuni did not dedicate his life simply to helping us to become completely enlightened and to escape the world of karma and rebirth. He taught us, rather, to teach others to teach others, until such time as the world is full of beings whose sole aim in life is to be of service to others. Thus, to arouse the thought of enlightenment is not just to make a determination to enlighten all beings; it is the determination to motivate all living beings to motivate all living beings, on and on. "Benefiting living beings," says Dōgen, "means causing living beings to arouse the thought of emancipating all others even before each is himself emancipated. We cannot become Buddhas in any other way than through the power of causing this thought [of emancipating all others before oneself is emancipated] to arise in others."[29] Thus, Dōgen universalizes the bodhisattva vow and the thought of enlightenment; his vision is that of a world in which all beings are motivated by this vow. It cannot be otherwise, according to him, for if any being enters the Dharma for himself, and not for others, it is not the Dharma and he has not entered. To practice the Dharma is to "drop off mind and body," and when mind and body have been forgotten to the extent that we are no longer selfishly motivated to acquire even the wonderful prize of enlightenment for ourselves, we have really entered the Dharma, really aroused the thought of enlightenment.

This arousing of the thought of enlightenment is then expressed in countless ways, all of which are "wonderful practice" based on this deeper consciousness. Consequently, the thought of enlightenment opens us up to, and frees us to, many activities that were impossible before. Because events are known by the enlightened mind itself, we no longer approach experience in the ordinary greedy or fearful manner. For the most part, this enlightened activity takes the form of gratitude to the Buddha and a desire to give to others whatever is within one's power to give.

Dōgen writes in *Hotsu mujō shin,*

It is the enlightened mind that arouses the thought of enlightenment. The meaning of this phrase, "it is the enlightened mind that arouses the thought of enlightenment," is that one makes a stupa with a blade of grass; one makes a sutra scroll with a rootless tree; one honors the Buddha with a grain of sand; one honors the Buddha with a bowl of water in which rice has been soaked.

One gives a handful of food to a living being, or offers five flowers to the Tathāgata. These are all forms of arousing the thought of enlightenment. Arousing the thought of enlightenment means following the encouragement of others, doing good even to the slight extent you are able, and bowing to the Buddha even while you are being annoyed by demons.

Furthermore, arousing the thought of enlightenment means knowing that your home is not your true home; it means leaving the home life, entering the mountains and practicing the Buddha Way, and practicing with faith in a teacher or the scriptures. It means making an image of the Buddha, building a stupa, reading the scriptures, being mindful of the Buddha, preaching the Dharma to living beings, visiting a teacher and asking questions, and sitting cross-legged doing zazen.[30]

Why are all these activities the same as arousing the thought of enlightenment? As Dōgen defines it, arousing the thought of enlightenment is truly a momentous affair. Yet, here it is said to be the same as doing zazen, offering someone a morsel of food, or offering flowers to the Buddha.

Why this is so will be clearer if we reflect on how hard it is now for us to do these things. It is hard for ordinary people to give rather than take. It is hard to perform what seem to be inherently meaningless acts such as bowing or offering incense to the Buddha. Zazen itself is hard because we do not really believe we can gain anything from it; it is lost time and often not much fun. The person who can easily do these things looks at life in a different way than most people do, for he can now do things without weighing them in terms of profit and loss. He has aroused the thought of enlightenment, which means he gives what he is capable of giving, whatever that may be, and he honors the Buddha and shows his gratitude in many ways. It is therefore true that to honor the Buddha with whatever poor thing one has and to give freely to others without any thought of benefit or loss is a sure sign that one has aroused the thought of enlightenment.

This arousing is faith, because both faith and arousing the thought of enlightenment bespeak an unshakable trust in the truth and value of the Buddha's teaching and a determination to live one's life in conformity with that teaching. It is also identical with home departure, for real home departure is a complete renunciation of fame, fortune, power, and security, and a new orientation toward the Buddha and his teaching. Thus, arousing the thought of enlightenment, faith, and home departure are all forms of what Dōgen calls "dropping off mind and body."

We can go through all the proper motions, doing Zen in a formalistic way, but it is not enough. It is clear that Dōgen has an extremely rigorous definition of what it means to follow the Dharma. We can shave our heads, burn mountains of incense, give up sex, meat, and alcohol, and sit on a meditation pillow until it crumbles to dust, but if we have not genuinely aroused the thought of enlightenment, we are still mountains and rivers away from the Dharma. If, however, in the perception of impermanence and suffering, one turns one's back on ordinary values, turns to the Buddha and his teachings as the real refuge of oneself and others, and places foremost in one's life the task of guiding all beings to enlightenment even before oneself is enlightened, then one has aroused the thought of enlightenment and truly entered the endless Path. The Buddha within has awakened, stretched, arisen, and gone forth to do his life's work.

Karma

KARMA literally means "act," "deed," "a doing." We can escape
neither karma nor its consequences. One of the oldest Buddhist texts, the *Dhammapada,* says that pain follows karma as the
plow follows the footprints of the ox. This is a very old teaching in
Buddhism, and it is accurate to say that the system of ideas and
practices of Buddhism, throughout its twenty-five centuries, has
been concerned mainly with the issue of karma. Zen itself is a Buddhist means of dealing with karma and its consequences.

Karma is defined in Buddhism as volitional action, meaning any
act, good or bad, that is preceded by will or intention. The act may
be a physical one, such as giving a gift; or a vocal one, such as lying;
or even a mental one, such as thinking angry thoughts; but if the act
is preceded by an intention, be it to give a gift or to lie, then karma
has occurred. Intentional acts are almost always motivated by either
desire or hatred, which are thus the content of the intention. Even
a desire to do good is still motivated by desire. Buddhism teaches
that an act that expresses desire or hatred leaves an impression or
residue in the mind (and here it is important to recall Dōgen's con-
cept of mind, expressed in *Hotsu mujō shin,* as absolute mind, as
including oneself and the whole world, unbound by time and
space). At some later time, this residue will bring about some result
or consequence in the life of the doer or in the lives of others. The
essential psychological insight of Buddhism is that we are unable to
perform acts of any nature without their having some influence on
our lives. Volitional acts are a form of energy that radiates outward

from the doer and affects both self and others. A murderer, for example, may never be apprehended and punished by civil authorities, but the deed survives in the present, and sometime, somewhere, the energy of the past act will have an effect on both the murderer and others. The energy is never lost.

It is human to act out of desire and loathing and thus to create unwholesome karma. However, karma is also created by those factors in our lives for which we are not personally responsible—that is, the many conditions we are each subject to by virtue of existing in a world of other entities. These conditions are countless and all affect our lives to one degree or another. They include the economic system of our society and the larger world, the quality of our minds, the bodies we have inherited from our parents, the food we eat, education, other people, and so on. In fact, every entity in the universe conditions our own personal existence in some way. Because of this, we are subject to many limitations; we can never exceed the intellectual capacity of our brains, for instance, nor, as living things, can we be free from sickness, pain, or old age. These things are our common lot as conditioned beings; they come to us despite our loathing of them, and like the karma mentioned earlier, they are with us wherever we go. The real question is how to deal effectively with those things that come to us whether we like them or not. "Flowers fall, giving rise to longing," says Dōgen, "and weeds flourish, arousing our loathing."

Religion also may be seen as one response to the fact of our limitations. Many people live lives of fear and insecurity and the acts they perform are really reactions to perceived threats against their security. So too can much pathological behavior be seen as a response to the realization that we cannot really ward off the invaders of our security. We realize that the weapons we employ in this battle are ineffective. In fact, all weapons are ineffective in the end. What, then, can we do?

In *Shunjū* ("Spring and Fall"), one of the essays from *Shōbōgenzō* translated in this volume, Dōgen addresses this problem of cause and effect. A monk approaches the Zen master Tung-shan and asks, "When the heat of summer and the cold of winter arrive, how can we escape them?" His question is, "How can we escape old age, sickness, death?" Tung-shan replies, "Why don't you go some place where there is no heat or cold?" "Where is this place where there is no heat or cold?" asks the monk. Tung-shan answers, "When it is hot, the heat kills the monk; when it is cold, the cold kills the monk." Now, the monk accepts the fact that the heat and cold will come. There is no chance that they will not. We will be hot in summer and cold in winter, whether we like it or not. Yet Tung-shan says that there is a place where there is neither heat nor cold. The question every Zen student seeks to answer through zazen is, "Where is this place where there is no heat or cold?"

The answer to this question takes many forms. One Zen master said, "When it is hot, fan yourself, and when it is cold, get closer to the heater." This seems to be a practical way of solving the problem, but Dōgen says that it is the answer of a child, because in the reality of life and death there are no equivalent fans or heaters. All the chemicals and machinery of medical science will only temporarily ward off eventual deterioration and death. Childish solutions to problems are not only ineffective but often compound the problem, yet people typically attack the matter of life and death as if they were still children.

Tung-shan says that there is a "place," however, where there is no heat or cold. It is a place where even though it is mid-summer and we perspire heavily, we are truly free from the heat; when we are free from the heat even as we are drenched with perspiration, we have found Tung-shan's place of no heat or cold. The bodhisattva who is willing, even eager, to be reborn forever in the realms of suffering and karmic effects has found this place right in the very midst of turmoil, anxiety, frustration, competition, terror, death, and all the rest.

This is why Zen Buddhism is truly a human religion, because it does not attempt to distract us from the reality of sentient existence by promising a future nirvana or heaven that is exempt from the conditions of sentient life. Rather, it demands that we see our lives with clear vision and find freedom and perfect goodness within and through the conditions that make up their fabric. Buddhism demands that we abandon all self-deception, all myths and daydreams, all beguiling fairy stories that prevent us from truly understanding the nature of our lives. There is, finally, only *this,* as the Zen master

Ta-mei told his students as he lay dying and heard a squirrel chatter on the roof. The blossoms fall despite our longing; the weeds flourish despite our loathing—and what can we do about it?

In *Shinjin inga* ("Deep Faith in Cause and Effect"), also translated in this volume, Dōgen concerns himself with this question. The essay begins with one of the best-known and most important kōans, "Pai-chang and the Fox." Every day when the Zen master Pai-chang spoke to the monks in the lecture hall, an old man would listen with them and then depart when they departed. One day, when the monks went out, the old man remained behind. "Who are you?" asked Pai-chang. "I am not human," answered the old man, "I am a fox spirit. Long ago, I was the abbot of a monastery on this spot. One day, a monk asked me, 'Is an enlightened person subject to the law of cause and effect?' and I answered, 'Such a person is not.' As a result of that, I have been reborn as a fox for five hundred lifetimes. Please say something now that will free me from the body of the fox. Is the enlightened individual subject to the law of cause and effect?" Pai-chang answered, "Such a person is not exempt from the law of cause and effect." Thereupon, the old man told Pai-chang that he was now freed from the body of the fox and requested that the fox's body be buried with the honors due a monk. Pai-chang said he would, and later he and the other monks found the fox's body and disposed of it properly.

Dōgen speaks approvingly of Pai-chang's answer, for the whole essay is a sustained assertion of the reality and inflexibility of the law of cause and effect. No one is exempt, not even abbots and Zen masters. Dōgen goes on to make the point that even after being freed from the body of the fox, the old man would have to be reborn in another realm, because there is no relaxation of the law of cause and effect. Dōgen's approval of Pai-chang's answer seems to reaffirm the fact of conditionedness for all entities, living and otherwise. Even the enlightened individual perspires in summer and shivers in winter, gets toothaches that hurt terribly, and grows old, in the end, like everyone else does. Perhaps even an enlightened individual may become a fox.

Then why practice and follow the Dharma? If both the enlightened person and the deluded fool end up as ashes and become foxes, why devote one's entire life to hard discipline and the pursuit of something called enlightenment? The reason is that Zen does promise that there is a "place" where we can be free from the toothache, the loss, the old age and death, even as we deeply experience the pain, the aging process, and the dying. Tung-shan says, "When it is hot, the heat kills the monk; when it is cold, the cold kills the monk." This statement is sometimes translated from the Japanese as, "When it is hot, be completely hot; when it is cold, be completely cold." In other words, instead of vainly seeking to escape the conditions that constitute our lives by means of flight—spiritual or otherwise—one finds a real and meaningful freedom from this conditionedness through a radical affirmation of one's very conditionedness. Thus, as Dōgen tells us in various places, when you are alive, be completely alive, and when you are dying, die thoroughly. This is in fact the lesson one learns in the *jijuyū zammai* that Dōgen praises so strongly. By means of an absolute oneness with the circumstances themselves, no matter what they are, one paradoxically becomes free from them. Dōgen calls this *gūjin*, a difficult term to translate, but which means something like "total realization," "total understanding," "total manifestation," or "total exertion." Looked at from the angle of the person who experiences a situation, it means that one identifies with it utterly. Looked at from the standpoint of the situation itself, the situation is totally manifested or exerted without obstruction.

There is another old Zen story that illustrates this total oneness with circumstances. A young monk was disillusioned with Zen when he heard his revered master scream in pain and fear as he was being murdered by thieves. The young man contemplated leaving Zen training, feeling that if his old master screamed in the face of pain or death, Zen itself must be a fraud. However, before he was able to leave, another teacher taught him something of what Zen is all about and removed his misconceptions. "Fool!" exclaimed the teacher, "the object of Zen is not to kill all feelings and become anesthetized to pain and fear. The object of Zen is to free us to scream loudly and fully when it is time to scream." This is Dōgen's *gūjin*, the total exertion of any circumstance. "When one side is illuminated," says Dōgen, "the other side is darkened." That is to say, when one becomes hot or cold, glad or griefstricken, completely, with nothing added, then being *nothing but* pain, heat, cold, grief, or joy (the "other side is darkened"), one has found Tungshan's place where there is neither heat nor cold. What is not added to the circumstance is the self, with its discriminations and judgments. How else can we be free from conditions?

Dōgen's Zen is a profound approach to the problem of life and death, yet there is no sign of mystical transcendence in this Zen (unless we call it "self-transcendence"). Rather, Dōgen's Zen immerses the individual even more deeply into the flow of worldly existence, affirming and transforming worldly experience itself, and completely rejecting the dualisms, implicit or explicit, in mystical and ordinary experience. There is no distinction between things that are holy and nonholy, worldly and nonworldly, sacred and profane, and consequently there are no transcendental realms into which one merges, leaving a presumably fallen and impure world behind. Dōgen's Zen can appear completely ordinary. We can recall the words of Bodhidharma again when he was asked by the Emperor Wu what the holy teaching of Buddhism is: "Vast emptiness, and nothing holy about it." What, after all, do the ancestral masters do? "Eat rice and drink tea," says Dōgen in *Kajō*.

However, there is eating rice and there is eating rice; the ordinary daily experience of the Zen masters, while apparently no different from our own, has been in fact transformed. Dōgen's Zen is a radically realistic solution to the problem of samsara, for instead of trying to go beyond the world, the individual learns to resee and renew worldly experience itself. In traditional Buddhist terminology, this reseeing and renewal are the realization that all of existence is the Buddha. The Buddha is everything—loss and failure, betrayal, the falling of flower petals, brain tumors, the hanged criminal, the collapse of dynasties, and the extinguishing of suns. There is no other reality, no matter how much we may long for one and dream of it. Therefore, there is no place to which to escape nor would there be any need to escape if such a place did exist, for we can, with determination and effort, see and understand this reality in such a way that we can affirm it just as it is. To do this, we must understand what our life is, as well as that larger life of which ours is only a part.

What is it, then? A chant used in a Zen ceremony says,

> The whole universe is an ocean of dazzling light,
> And on it dance the waves of life and death.

What does it mean that the whole universe is an ocean of dazzling light? Why is it so difficult to see that light? How can we learn to see it?

Again, the object of practice is not transcendence but transformation, and yet ultimately we must transcend ourselves. It is the insistent intrusion of the self and its needs that causes our suffering. However, this self-transcendence does not mean removing ourselves from this reality, getting out of the stream of cause and effect and the process of action and consequence. Enlightenment may not literally free us from rebirth, as it did not the old man who spoke to Pai-chang. He was reborn after being freed from the body of the fox, but what fate may have lain in store for him, attached as he was to having human form and disliking his foxness? Zen does not guarantee that we will escape such karmic possibilities, but it does guarantee that with diligent effort we can come to see that there is nothing wrong with being a fox. May not the five hundred lives that the old abbot spent as a fox have been delightful? Does a fox regret his foxness and long to be a human, or is a fox just as perfect in his foxness as a human being is in his humanness? Master Mumon says in his commentary on "Pai-chang and the Fox" in the *Mumonkan* (case 2):

> "Not falling into causation." Why was he turned into a fox? "Not ignoring causation." Why was he released from the fox body? If you have an eye to see through this, then you will know that the former head of the monastery did enjoy his five hundred happy blessed lives as a fox.[31]

Pai-chang was certainly correct in saying that the enlightened individual is subject to the law of cause and effect. However, was the former abbot's comment really untrue, that an enlightened person is free from cause and effect? It is, if it means that the enlightened person cannot become a fox, but it is not if it means that the fox can enjoy his foxness and be free from it. Zen abbots die like everyone else, and even Shakyamuni grew old, suffered from dysentery, and then died from it. And yet, the enlightened individual is free from life and death through the very act of totally affirming and confirming life and death.

Every person who truly undertakes Zen training does so in the belief that there is something wrong with him or her, because the reality of our lives does not measure up to some idealized self-image that can be attained through spiritual training. Zen training shows us what we really are, our reality as distinct from the idealization. Then, with luck and hard work, we discover that what we really are is perfect and has been all along.

Scriptures

IN *Nyorai zenshin,* which is translated as "The Tathāgata's Whole Body," Dōgen is concerned with scriptural literature, with stupas —the funerary mounds that enclose the ashes of important Buddhist figures—and with the whole body of the Buddha. Yet this chapter is also about practice, as are all the chapters of *Shōbōgenzō* translated in this volume. Though about practice, it does not concern proper posture and the like, for the Zen practice of which Dōgen writes goes beyond formal zazen activities. *Nyorai zenshin,* in talking about stupas, sutras, and the essence of the Buddha, presents us with several important ideas that help orient us in our practice.

Dōgen tells us in *Nyorai zenshin* that the true remains of the Buddha's body are found in the sutras. It has been the custom in Buddhist countries ever since the time of Shakyamuni to cremate the dead, and the Buddha himself was cremated. Usually, all that remains of the body are a few small fragments of bone and some ashes, called *sharīra* and often referred to as "relics." They are considered to be the essence of the dead body, though not a metaphysical essence or self. These relics were frequently enshrined in a stupa, and presumably Shakyamuni's relics were enshrined in the same way. But the point that Dōgen makes in *Nyorai zenshin* is that the true relics do not consist of the ashes and bone entombed in the stupa, but of the teachings that are enshrined in the scriptures. Thus, the real body of Shakyamuni is the Dharma itself; the Dharma is the whole body of the Tathāgata.

One of the things that characterizes Dōgen's Zen is his attempt to restore the importance of the sutras by countering the tendency that arose in Chinese Zen to severely devalue them. Bodhidharma's "no dependence on words or letters" is either the source of this high-handed disregard of the scriptures or a later literary expression of it, but in any case, "no dependence on words or letters" has come to serve as an ideological basis for disparaging reading and learning. Bodhidharma's words, however, speak only of "dependence" on literature, not of reading it and verifying it for oneself. Bodhidharma does not counsel us to disregard and disrespect the sutras, but merely warns of depending on them. Early Chinese Zen was conscious of itself as constituting a radical departure from traditional Chinese Buddhism, which was oriented almost exclusively toward scriptural study, lecturing, exegesis, and writing learned commentaries. Pre-Zen and, later, non-Zen Buddhism therefore tended to be somewhat more academic and scholarly, with almost no emphasis on actual practice. Zen was a departure because it originated in the knowledge that practice and attainment, not theoretical knowledge and scholarship, are the real heart of Buddhism, and Bodhidharma's famous verse is an advertisement of the nature of this new Chinese Buddhism. A polemical view emerged in Zen that reading the scriptures is harmful. People holding this view spoke disparagingly of the scriptures, and seemed almost to behave as if the Buddha's words were like poisonous serpents. The familiar painting of Hui-neng gleefully tearing up a copy of the *Diamond Sutra* graphically portrays the excesses of this attitude. Clearly, if one does nothing but read the scriptures, this is not real Zen practice—and is not enlightenment—but careful study of them can enhance and strengthen true practice. For centuries both Chinese and Japanese Zen monastic compounds contained libraries, bespeaking the value of scriptures and study.

Dōgen attempts to restore the importance of the scriptures when he asserts that the sutra itself is the whole body of the Buddha. To understand this assertion, we need to understand the question behind it: "Where can the whole body of the Buddha *not* be found?" We see in *Nyorai zenshin* that when the Buddha instructs the bodhisattva Bhaisajyarāja to venerate a stupa, he says that the relics of the Buddha need not be placed in it, because it already contains the whole body of the Buddha—the whole body is everywhere. In fact, the whole body of the Tathāgata is enshrined in each entity, and thus the relics do not need to be placed in the stupa. Indeed, they *cannot* be.

It is clear from *Nyorai zenshin* that for Dōgen the scriptures were both the voice of the Buddha and the Buddha himself, for he says that we pay homage to the Buddha when we pay homage to the sutra. As such, he says, we should "accept it, support it, read and recite it, explain, preach, and copy it, and in so doing become enlightened." Can we truly become enlightened in this way? Hui-neng became enlightened merely by hearing someone recite a portion of the *Diamond Sutra*. And Hui-neng is not unique in being awakened by scripture, for the records of Buddhist priests show that several were enlightened while reading the sutras. But admittedly, few achieve it in this way. Long before we truly understand that all things are empty (as the texts teach), a deep, meditative reading of a Buddhist text such as the *Diamond Sutra* must take place. That in itself may not be enlightenment, but it is something valuable.

However, it is not only the sutra pages with their words in black print that are the whole body of the Buddha, for Dōgen tells us that the acts of reading and writing are themselves also the whole body of the Buddha. All our activities are Buddha activities—and this includes intellectual activity. Even thinking and reasoning are Buddha activities.

This is important to keep in mind as we undertake Zen practice, because otherwise, we can easily fall into the error of assuming that there are only certain special places and activities in which the whole body of the Buddha can be found. We need to remember further that Zen practice itself has as its goal the overcoming of a false dualistic view whereby we discriminate between things that are worthy and unworthy, sacred and profane, good and bad, Buddha and non-Buddha. We forget that the whole universe is the stupa that contains the whole body of the Buddha. Consequently the Buddha is found everywhere: in other people—even the ones we do not like very much; in crowded, noisy cities, not just in the country with frogs and crickets; in the kitchen full of dirty dishes; in the fussing child; and, to be sure, in the scriptures and other literature. In forgetting this and entwining ourselves ever more deeply with duality and discrimination, we do not really practice Zen.

It is not that just a fragment of the Buddha is to be found in the kitchen, or in the scriptures, or in the screams of the man dying in pain; each is the whole body of the Buddha just as it is, and each preaches the Dharma clearly and wholly. Dōgen says in *Raihai tokuzui* that rocks and trees preach the Dharma, and that we can hear it preached by pillars, walls, and hedges. The Hua-yen School's master Fa-tsang said that ten thousand Buddhas preach the Dharma on the tip of a hair. For Dōgen, this means that the Dharma is also fully manifest in the scriptures.

Dōgen tells us that the sutra pages with their words in black print are the whole body of the Buddha. Furthermore, it is not just sitting in the meditation hall, wreathed with incense smoke, calm and passionless, that is Buddha, but also reading, writing, copying, teaching, and paying homage to the scriptures. All our activities are Buddha activities—including our intellectual activity. The purpose of Zen practice is to actualize the total individual—mind, feelings, physical organism, will. Buddhism has never negated intellectual activity per se but only deluded thinking and frivolous study in place of direct experience.

For Dōgen, the scriptures, as much as zazen, have the power to help us realize our own Buddhahood. This is true also of koans, Hua-yen philosophy, and *Shōbōgenzō*. We may even think of these works as bodhisattvas, in the same way that Tibetan Buddhists rightly think of their *tanka* paintings as bodhisattvas, insofar as their compassionate activity fills us with faith and confidence, educates us, and inspires us to see the truth that they embody and teach. Thus, Dōgen says that we pay homage to the Buddha when we pay homage to the sutra. As the Buddha's whole body, we should "accept it, support it, read and recite it, explain, preach, and copy it, and in so doing become enlightened."

The true goal of Buddhism is not mere "spiritualization," but, as Dōgen says in *Hotsu bodai shin*, to save all sentient beings even before we ourselves are completely saved. Thus, service to others is the object of Zen practice. Our practice is a means of equipping us to be able to give effectively, which is to say, selflessly and without delusion. In commenting on the spiritual perfections *(paramitas),* Buddhist writers have often pointed out that the most essential of these is the first, which is giving *(dana).* Giving takes several forms, including material things: food, money, medicine—and the Dharma itself. But how can a person give the Dharma or try to save all beings if he is almost entirely ignorant of what the Dharma is? To give and serve implies first of all that we have something to give. Materially, we need only give what little we have, however small it is. But to give the Dharma requires that we prepare ourselves in two ways: first, we must do zazen and make ourselves fit vessels for the Dharma; and second, we must learn the Buddhist tradition through reading and study and thereby have the most complete Dharma to impart.

Zazen and study complement and strengthen each other. A good Buddhist practice would ideally combine zazen with a deep, careful study of Buddhist thought and practice. This has been the tradition of Tibetan Buddhism from its inception, and it has produced people who embodied (and still embody today) the admirable fruits of both meditation and study. Zazen experience enables the individual to have a much deeper understanding of doctrines than if study were pursued without the formal meditation; at the same time, by helping us develop a subtle understanding and deep appreciation for the beauty, subtlety, and power of the scriptures, the Buddhist teachings can help to guide, strengthen, and inspire our zazen practice.

Giving Life to Our Lives

WE HAVE NOTHING but our lives here and now as we live them from moment to moment. The past as an actuality is gone, and exists, if at all, only as memory and condition. The future does not exist at all, except as potentiality and possibility. There is no other, better place to be than where we are right now. If this place and situation are vexing to the spirit, the problem is within ourselves, not inherent in the place or situation.

The Zen of Dōgen is a way of dealing with the fact that we find ourselves, always, in a certain time, in a certain body, living a certain kind of life along with certain other lives. And Dōgen tells us to live life fully, to give life to our lives. The everyday life of the Zen master consists merely of eating rice and drinking tea. An enlightened individual is one who has learned to give life to—not kill—ordinary acts like these. "Eating rice and drinking tea" means, of course, the whole ordinary, everyday life. We can kill our lives in many ways. We can kill them by living them in a semi-stupor, in unawareness, mechanically, as if we were drugged. And, we can kill them by discriminating, devaluing, and demeaning, which occurs when we wish for other situations that we consider more valuable than the ones we are in. To yearn for lobster and fine wine while having plain rice and tea is to discriminate against the rice and tea, to kill the rice and tea and one's experience of them. To want to be in some other place is to kill this place. To want to be entertained instead of working is to kill work. Giving life to each moment is understanding that what we are, what we do, and where we do it are good enough. They are more than good enough; they are perfect.

There is a haiku by Bashō:

Lice, fleas,
The horse pissing
Beside my pillow.

Bashō had been wandering about Japan, as he liked to do, and found himself at nightfall with no place to spend the night except in a stable. As he tried to sleep, he felt lice and fleas begin to crawl over him and heard (and perhaps felt also!) the nearby horse relieve itself. Bashō's recreating this moment does not contain self-pity, anger, disgust, or irritation. There is, in fact, no judgment, no aversion at all, and even the poet himself is absent from the poem. Bashō merely reports the moment as it is and presumably goes to sleep. This ability to enter into a moment completely, without judgment, without condemning the present or yearning for a non-existent alternative, is living the lives of the Buddhas and ancestors; this is giving life to our life.

In *Kajō* ("Daily Life"), Dōgen tells us that to live our lives as the constant actualization of our inherent enlightenment is simply to eat rice and drink tea. But we so rarely simply do this. We can lose a whole lifetime by dwelling on where we were in the past or where we wish to be in the future. We imagine that enlightenment involves spectacular feats such as levitation, or walking on water, or reading the minds of others. Or we may imagine some kind of transformation into a saintly figure draped in flowing robes, perhaps emitting an aura, uttering holy words, and swaying entire crowds with solemn, authoritative pronouncements of Truth. Yet Dōgen says that enlightenment is just eating rice and drinking tea, that simple acts like these are indeed marvellous and are manifestations of the enlightened life of the ancestors.

What makes such ordinary acts marvellous is that they are *total*. Yün-yen and Tao-wu, two Zen monks, were talking one day, and Yün-yen asked Tao-wu, "Why does Avalokiteshvara have so many hands and eyes?" Tao-wu replied, "It is like a person who gropes behind himself in the night, searching for his pillow." "I understand! I understand!" cried Yün-yen. "What do you understand?" Tao-wu asked. Replied Yün-yen, "The whole body is covered with hands and eyes." "Not bad, not bad," Tao-wu said, "you have expressed it pretty well." "That's as well as I can do," said Yün-yen. "How about you, elder brother?" Tao-wu answered, "The whole body is hands and eyes." Images of Avalokiteshvara with their many arms and many heads portray the essence of enlightenment as absolute, unqualified, compassionate activity. Total acts are performed not merely with one or two hands, or even a hundred or a million hands, but with an infinity of hands—performed by one who is just hands. Thus even an act as ordinary as eating is performed with total exertion, without omitting even a fragment of oneself from the act. This is what Dōgen means by *gūjin.*

The essay called *Gyōji* ("Continuous Practice") is a long description of the daily lives of the ancestral masters from the time of Shakyamuni almost down to the time of Dōgen himself. These stories are almost completely devoid of the saintly, the miraculous, or the supernatural. Instead, we see clearly that all these persons led ordinary—though active and creative—lives. Story after story is much the same: each master, when he himself was a student, studied with his own master, eventually realized his own awakened nature, and continued for the rest of his life to manifest this awakening in all his daily actions. Lin-chi planted cedars for the benefit of future generations, Pai-chang worked in the fields with his students well into old age, and Ta-an ate rice and raised an ox.

Dōgen calls this activity *gyōji. Gyō* is activity, performance, and training. It is not just any activity but activity illuminated by understanding. *Ji* means "to maintain," "to hold on to." *Gyōji* is activity in which we constantly make a strong effort to see and live our daily lives as continous Zen training. It is thus a life of desirelessness, without preferences, without picking and choosing. When the activities of ordinary life—just eating, drinking, working, sleeping—are undertaken as manifestations of insight, we are content with what we are, where we are, and what we must do. Consequently, we live always here, now, in this place, in this particular way, entering totally into each act without reservations or conditions, always realizing, actualizing, giving life to the simple beads of experience we call "now." This *gyōji,* consequently, is none other than living life with the thousand hands and eyes of Avalokiteshvara.

Dōgen Zenji says in *Gyōji* that continous practice is always now, for the nature of continuous practice is such that it cannot exist either in the past or in the future. To be in the past or future mentally while we are physically in the present means that there is a dividedness in our lives, a lack of complete centeredness. Memory and fantasy in themselves are harmless, but they become a problem when they prevent us from occupying the present, which is all we will ever really have.

What is this "now"? It is not really the "now" of time, which is the sliver-thin juncture between the past and future, although it may help to think of "now" that way. If "now" is the pure immediacy of lived experience in each event, then each "now" ceases and becomes memory, to be replaced by an entirely new "now," in a process that goes on forever. Hence, there is a stream of "nows," following one another, not as units of time but as just totally lived beads of experience. The totally lived experience of one "now" is unique; it does not guarantee that the next moment will be lived in the same fashion. Consequently, to practice continously means to make a constant effort to awaken, over and over, as each new experience arises. It is to be constantly actualizing our enlightened nature anew in each event, moment after moment.

The whole universe is an ocean of dazzling light, according to a line in the memorial service *(gakki)* recited in the Dharma hall on the occasion of remembering and honoring our spiritual ancestors. We need to proceed in our practice in the faith that the whole universe is indeed an ocean of dazzling light, the very body of the Buddha. Then we can find that light everywhere, in every event, in every new "now." Eating plain rice and drinking tea are part of this ocean of light. The task of the individual who trains in Zen is to learn to see this. This itself is Zen practice.

How ordinary, plain, and simple Zen is! It is a life with one's feet on the ground of one's native home, toes buried in the fragrant dirt. It is a life of appreciation for the wonderful taste of boiled rice and green tea. It is a life of bowing continually to the Buddha, whose face is seen shining from every entity, every event. Through this continuous practice, we give life to our lives.

Concerning the Translation

IT IS CUSTOMARY for translators of Dōgen's writings to say something about how difficult it is to translate his works and to modestly disclaim any hopes for a perfect translation. I would like to take this opportunity to join them. I believe that I have succeeded by and large in being accurate, and have made every effort to ensure that Dōgen does not say something in English that he never said in Japanese. The reader may therefore proceed in the confidence that the following pages reasonably represent the original Japanese, but undoubtedly they are not perfect.

The truth of the matter is that Dōgen's writings are very difficult, even for a person who reads Japanese with some ease. Most Japanese who write about Dōgen themselves say this. There are several reasons why this literature is so difficult. First, the literary form of Japanese has changed considerably since the time of Dōgen. Expressions current in the thirteenth century have completely dropped out of usage, meanings of other terms have changed, and there is less of a tendency now to incorporate lengthy Chinese phrases into a Japanese sentence. Dōgen wrote in Japanese, but frequently he incorporated whole sentences or extended passages in Sung Chinese, with its own syntax, without the grammatical particles that make the Japanese clearer. Also, he tended to leave out these elements of syntax even when writing Japanese, a custom of his time but one that sometimes makes a sentence hard to construe grammatically. Colloquial expressions, of which the Chinese masters were so fond, abound in *Shōbōgenzō*, and their meaning can often be found only after consulting special dictionaries and glossaries. Some are not even recorded.

These expressions are also difficult to translate exactly and smoothly into English, and while I have tried to arrive at a translation that is as close to the original as I could make it, at times a term, a phrase, or a whole sentence had to be paraphrased. In these cases, literal translation is not possible, and the best a translator can hope for is a sense of the original. For example, a Japanese sentence such as *itonamu koto nakare* can be exactly translated, without paraphrase or loss of literalism, as "Do not do it." But consider the term *zushin bishin,* which occurs in the *Kannon* chapter of *Shōbō-genzō: zu* means "head," *bi* means "tail," and *shin* here means "correct," "upright," "perfect," "true," "orthodox," and "straight." Thus the term literally means something like "head perfect, tail perfect." But the sentence in which it occurs would then literally read, "Are they [one's own hands and eyes] merely one or two pieces of the head perfect tail perfect hands and eyes?" Furthermore, this old term is said in several dictionaries to mean "from beginning to end," or "perfect from start to finish." But this does not seem to fit into the sentence either. After considerable research, one discovers that it means something like "absolute." Thus, what Dōgen is asking is whether one's own hands and eyes are merely one or two pieces of the absolute—or absolutely manifested—hands and eyes of Avalo-kiteshvara Bodhisattva. And in context, this makes sense. My point is twofold: first, the text of *Shōbōgenzō* is extremely difficult for any translator. Second, despite a sustained attempt to keep as literally close to Dōgen's own manner of expression as possible, sometimes a paraphrase or otherwise nonliteral rendition is required and is inescapable if the English version is to make any sense at all.

Another difficulty arises from the fact that *Shōbōgenzō* is a Zen text, and I doubt that any other religious literature is quite like it. Zen writers, especially those of early Chinese and Japanese Zen, do not express themselves in conventional, everyday language, or do not use that language in the common sense. First, their expression tends to be very concrete instead of abstract. Thus, when asked "What is the Buddha?" a Zen master will reply, "The cypress tree in the courtyard," instead of involving you in a discussion about "immanence," "absolute," "reality," "emptiness," or "truth." Also, because they do not see ordinary things in an ordinary way, their behavior and expression are often unconventional and unpredictable. This presents another problem for the translator. Even after individual words and phrases are deciphered and the syntax is solved, the resulting English sentence is frequently so bizarre that the translator cannot be sure that the translation is correct. Confidence comes only with some degree of familiarity with the special world of Zen literature.

A related problem in the translation of *Shōbōgenzō* concerns the fact that Dōgen himself was not an ordinary man in certain ways. He addresses the reader from a level of great spiritual insight, and the reader's challenge is to try to comprehend Dōgen's vision from Dōgen's own vantage point. Dōgen is difficult to follow because he sees a reality we do not even vaguely imagine. This is a real problem for the translator because no matter how learned one is in reading ancient Chinese and Japanese texts, in understanding complex Buddhist doctrines, or in the history of Buddhism, the point of a passage will sometimes be missed because the translator, not having attained Dōgen's insight, simply does not understand what Dōgen is saying.

This problem is further deepened by the fact that Dōgen was also a poet with a deep sensitivity to language. He used words carefully and precisely, and consequently the nuances of words are very important. The translator must struggle to find as exact an equivalent to Dōgen's terminology as possible. When these nuances are obliterated by a general paraphrase of the original, something crucial has been lost. This is particularly true in the great many instances in which Dōgen carefully discusses the terminology of some kōan.

Another problem is related to the fact that Dōgen spoke authoritatively about life from the standpoint of an enlightened person. Because he saw reality in a certain way, he tended to make conventional language and traditional Buddhist literature serve this vision in a most original and striking fashion. A well-known example is his reading of the passage in the *Mahāpāranirvāna Sutra* that says, "All sentient beings possess Buddha nature." Convinced as he was that there are not two separate realities, beings and Buddha, but rather that all things, including nonsentient beings, are Buddha just as they are, he reads the passage as saying, "All existence is Buddha nature." Throughout *Shōbōgenzō,* language is adapted to serve the truth as Dōgen saw it.

Thus, translating *Shōbōgenzō* is a difficult task. The ideal translator of this literature, in my view, would be a person who knew thirteenth-century Japanese well, was sensitive to language in general, was well trained in the history, practices, and doctrines of Buddhism, and approached the text in the light of personal Zen practice. I feel that this last requirement is very important, because unless the translator has experiential insight into what Dōgen is saying, much in the text will be missed and the translation will suffer.

I also believe that despite all the difficulties of *Shōbōgenzō,* it is possible to translate it in such a way that the considerable power and beauty of the original can be retained. I agree that in some instances only a paraphrase is possible, but for the most part the English version can faithfully reflect the original. I have tried to keep this in mind at all times while translating the text, for it is my feeling that *Shōbōgenzō* is one of the most remarkable pieces of world literature and as such deserves all the care and attention one can give it.

Finally, a few words about procedures. First, I have written Chinese personal and place names in the Chinese pronunciation instead of in the more familiar Japanese pronunciation by which they are usually known to scholars and practitioners of Japanese Zen. As a result of this, the reader will find *Hui-neng* instead of the more familiar *Eno,* *Huang-po* instead of *Obaku,* and so on. If the Chinese names themselves are translations or transliterations of Indian names, I have restored the name to the Indian original. Thus, for example, the reader will find *Avalokiteshvara* instead of *Kuan-yin* (or the Japanese *Kannon*). The geneology chart at the back of the book will clarify the correspondences between Chinese names and their Japanese counterparts.

These translations could not have been done without the help of Japanese scholars whose reference works and translations of Dōgen's writings into modern Japanese have helped me at every step of the way. Some of the more important works are listed below.

1. *Shōbōgenzō shisō taikei,* by Okada Gihō. Modern Japanese translation with commentary.

2. *Shōbōgenzō sankyū,* by Yasutani Hakuun Roshi. Invaluable and illuminating commentary by a contemporary Zen master.

3. *Zenyaku shōbōgenzō,* by Nakamura Soichi. Very good translation of *Shōbōgenzō* into modern Japanese. His dictionary of expressions in *Shōbōgenzō,* the *Shōbōgenzō yōgo jiten,* has been indispensable.

4. *Shōbōgenzō chūkai zensho,* by Jimbo Nyoten and Andō Bun'ei. A collection of some of the best-known and most authoritative older commentaries on *Shōbōgenzō.*

I have also benefited from other Western translations, particularly the following:

1. *Dōgen Kigen: Mystical Realist,* by Hee-jin Kim.

2. *Zen Master Dōgen,* by Yūhō Yokoi and Daizen Victoria.

3. Various chapters of *Shōbōgenzō,* translated by Abe Masao and Norman Waddell, which have appeared in recent issues of the journal *Eastern Buddhist.*

Translations

Fukan Zazengi

GENERAL RECOMMENDATIONS
FOR DOING ZAZEN

THE WAY is essentially perfect and exists everywhere. There is no need either to seek or to realize the Way. The Truth that carries us along is sovereign and does not require our efforts. Need I say that it excels this world? Who can believe that the expedient of [mirror-]wiping is necessary?[32] Essentially the Truth is very close to you; is it then necessary to run around in search of it?

Even so, if there is the slightest error, there is a gulf as great as that between heaven and earth. If so much as a thought of agreeable or disagreeable arises, one becomes confused. For instance, you may feel proud in your comprehension, or you may feel prosperous in achieving satori. Even if you acquire satori in the blink of an eye, acquire the Way and enlighten your mind, feel as if you could assault heaven itself, and charge into the Dharma as if on a mere saunter, you may shortly lose the way of dropping off the body.

How may one perceive the traces of that one of Jetavana [the Buddha], who saw all things as they truly are with his own enlightened nature and yet still did zazen for six years? The fame of that one of Shao-lin Temple [Bodhidharma], who transmitted the mind-seal [from India] and who for nine years still sat facing a wall [in meditation], is being transmitted even now. If this was true of the ancient worthies, people of today must also exert themselves.

For this reason, you must suspend your attempts to understand by means of scrutinizing words, reverse the activity of the mind that seeks externally, and illuminate your own true nature. Mind and body will fall off spontaneously, and your original face will be revealed. If you wish to achieve such a thing, you must exert yourself in this matter at once.

For zazen, you will need a quiet room. Eat and drink in moderation. Forget about the concerns of the day and leave such matters alone. Do not judge things as good or evil, and cease such distinctions as "is" and "is not." Halt the flow of the mind, and cease conceptualizing, thinking, and observing. Don't sit in order to become a Buddha, because becoming a Buddha has nothing to do with such things as sitting or lying down.

In the room that you use for zazen, spread some thick mats and place a firm, round pillow on them. Sit on the pillow with your legs crossed either in the full-lotus position or in the half-lotus position. This means [in the full-lotus position] that you place your right foot on your left thigh, and your left foot on your right thigh. In the half-lotus position, you just put your left foot on your right thigh [with the right foot on the mat beneath your left thigh].

Loosen your clothes and belt and arrange them neatly. Next, place your right hand [palm up] on top of your left foot, and place your left hand [palm up] in the palm of your right hand. Both thumb tips should touch slightly.

Now regulate your posture so you are sitting properly, leaning neither to the left nor to the right, forward nor backward. [Looked at from the side], your ears and shoulders should be in a straight line, and from the front, your nose will be in a direct line with your navel. Place your tongue against the roof of your mouth, and keep your teeth and lips closed. Your eyes should be [slightly] open, and your breathing should be soft.

When your body posture is correct, breathe in and out [once, deeply]. Sway left and right [several times] and then sit firmly and resolutely. Think about the unthinkable. How do you think about the unthinkable? Non-thinking. These are the essentials of zazen.

That which we call zazen is not a way of developing concentration. It is simply the comfortable way. It is practice that measures your satori to the fullest, and is in fact satori itself. It is the manifestation of the ultimate reality, and in it you will no longer be trapped as in a basket or a cage. If you understand my meaning [and do zazen correctly], you will be like a dragon who has reached the water, or like a tiger who trusts in the mountain where he dwells. Know that the true Dharma itself is present [in zazen], and that confusion and distraction are eradicated right from the beginning.

When you get up from zazen, move quietly and slowly. Do not make violent movements. When we contemplate the past, we observe that transcending both the sacred and the profane, or such things as dying while in zazen or while standing [which the old Zen masters did] came about through this power. It is even more difficult to explain with words and analysis how the ancient masters could seize upon the crucial moment that brought about satori in a disciple by pointing a finger, using the tip of a pole, a needle, or a mallet, and give encouragement with the *hossu*,[33] a fist, a stick, or a shout. How can supernatural powers explain practice and enlightenment? Practice and enlightenment are the majestic deportment of the body, beyond the sights and sounds [of this world]. What can they be other than the Dharma, which is prior to understanding and analysis?

Such being the case, there is no question here at all of being intelligent or stupid, nor is there any difference between the quick-witted and the dull. If you exert yourself single-mindedly, this is practicing the Way itself. Practice and realization leave not a trace of impurity, and the person who advances in the Way is an ordinary person.

This world or other worlds, India or China, all equally preserve the seal of the Buddha.[34] One who adheres exclusively to the customs of Zen practices zazen only, doing nothing but sitting resolutely on the ground. You may hear of ten thousand distinctions or a thousand differences,[35] but just do zazen earnestly and make an effort in the Way. You don't need to abandon your own sitting place and just for amusement go to some other country. If you err by a single step, you lose the Way.

Now you have acquired the essential, which is a human form. Do not pass over from the light to the shadow [by pursuing other matters]. Take care of this essential instrument of the Buddha's Way. Could you really be content with a spark from a stone [when the blazing sun is shining]? And that is not all; your body is like dew on the grass, your life is as brief as a flash of lightening. Momentary and vain, it is lost in an instant.

I entreat you who practice in the splendid tradition of Zen, do not grope around as if you were in a group of blind people or be in doubt when you see a real dragon.[36] Just persevere in the simple Way that has been indicated for you so directly. Value those beings who have perfected their own practice and have finished what was to be done. If you conform to the satori of all the Buddhas, you will become an heir to the samādhi of all the [Zen] ancestors. If you practice like this for a long time, you will surely become like them. The precious treasury will open its doors all by itself, and the treasure will be yours to use as you wish.

Keisei Sanshoku

"THE SOUNDS OF THE VALLEY STREAMS,

THE FORMS OF THE MOUNTAINS"

M ANY ARE the Buddha ancestors who have transmitted the supreme Way to the highest enlightenment and who have taught the methods of practice. The traces still remain of our predecessors who broke their bones in learning the Way. You should study the life of the second ancestor Hui-k'o, who cut off his arm in order to receive the teaching,[37] and do not be attached to even a single hair of your body. When you finally achieve the various liberations by doing zazen, everything that was withheld from you in the past because of your discriminating mind will be revealed to you at once. I do not understand this instant of revelation of reality, nor do you, nor does anyone else. Not even the Buddha vision sees it, so how can it be fathomed by human calculation?

There once lived a Chinese *upāsaka* [a lay adherent to the Buddhist precepts] named Tung-p'o,[38] whose family name was Su and whose official name was Shih. His courtesy name was Tzu-chan. He was a very famous man, a real dragon in the ocean of letters. It was said he studied the dragons and *nagas*[39] in the ocean of Buddhism. He sported freely in the depths [like a dragon] and rose up to the high-piled clouds. Once, on Mount Lu, he was enlightened when he heard the sound of valley streams flowing in the night. He composed a verse and presented it to Ch'an master Ch'ang Tsung. This was the verse:

sounds and forms

The sounds of the valley streams are his long, broad tongue;
The forms of the mountains are his pure body.

At night I heard the myriad sutra verses uttered
How can I relate to others what they say?

When he presented this verse to Master Tsung, the master approved it. He was the Ch'an master Chao-hsüeh Ch'ang-tsung, who was the Dharma heir of Ch'an master Huang-lung Hui-nan. Hui-nan himself was the Dharma heir of the Ch'an master Tz'u-ming Ch'u-yüan.

Later, this upāsaka met the Ch'an master Liao-yuan and at that time Liao-yuan gave him the precepts and robes. Thereafter, the upāsaka always put on the robes and did zazen. He respectfully presented Liao-yuan with a sash decorated with priceless jewels. People of that time said, "This sort of thing is not possible for ordinary people like us to do, he must be very unusual."

This being the case, how can we not consider the circumstances of Su Tung-p'o's hearing the valley streams and becoming enlightened to be a great benefit extending down to the present time? It is deplorable, but it is almost as if something were lacking in people's ability to understand the expounding of the Dharma in these boundless manifestations of the Buddha's body. If this revelation of the Buddha's body is the preaching of the Dharma, then how are people today to see the forms of the mountains and hear the sounds of the streams? Do they hear them as a single phrase? Are they just half a phrase? Are they myriad verses? How regrettable it is that there are sounds and forms in the streams and mountains that we cannot understand. Yet it is a matter for delight that we have the opportunity to acquire the proper conditions for experiencing the Way in these sounds and forms. The sounds are never stilled, and the forms never cease to exist. This being so, does this mean that when they are revealed the body is near and that when they are obscured the body is not near? Is it the whole body, or is it just half the body? Because the springs and autumns of former times have completely become mountains and streams, you cannot detect them in mountains and streams; because the times prior to this night have completely become mountains and streams, you can see them as mountains and streams. Today's bodhisattva who practices the Way should begin his study of the Way in the knowledge that the mountains flow and the stream does not flow.

As for that night when Su Tung-p'o was enlightened, he had, on the previous day, asked Master Tsung about the saying that even insentient things preach the Dharma, and while he had had no really significant experience from hearing the master's explanation, later that night when he heard the sound of the streams, it was as if the billowing waves touched the high heavens. When this occurred, the sound astonished the upāsaka. But should we say it was the sound of the streams, or should we rather say that it was the sound of Master Chao-hsüeh flowing? Perhaps Chao-hsüeh's discussion of the idea of insentient things preaching the Dharma had not really stopped, but was imperceptibly mixed with the night sounds of the valley streams. Now, someone might say that it was "a single water," or that it was the "ocean of oneness," the oneness of the water of the Dharma and the water of the streams. If we examine the matter closely, was it the upāsaka who became enlightened, or was it the mountains and streams that became enlightened? If anyone has eyes to see, then certainly anyone is able to see the long, broad tongue and the pure body.

When the Ch'an master Hsiang-yen Chih-hsien was practicing the Way under Ch'an master Ta-wei Ta-yuan, Ta-wei said to him, "You are quite bright and seem to understand everything. Without any reliance on your learned treatises, from what you were before your parents conceived you, give me one single phrase concerning the Way." Try as he might, Hsiang-yen could think of nothing to say in reply. He regretted his mind and body, and try as he might to find some clue in the books he had accumulated over many years, it was no use at all. So he set fire to all his precious books, saying, "A picture of rice cakes does not satisfy one's hunger. I will no longer seek the Buddha Way in this present life, and my practice will be that of serving the rice to practicing monks." So saying, he spent many years as a meal-serving monk. The expression, "meal-serving monk" refers to someone who serves rice and other food to the monks who are practicing.

One day, he spoke to Ta-wei: "My mind is clouded and I cannot speak; say something that will help me, Chief Priest!" Ta-wei replied, "Unfortunately, I cannot say anything for you; maybe later you would resent my having done so." So the years passed, and Hsiang-yen traveled to Wu-tang Mountain searching for the whereabouts of the national teacher, Ta-cheng, and near the hermitage of the national teacher he built a grass hut, which he used as his own hermitage. He planted some young bamboo nearby and spent his days in its vicinity. One day, when he was sweeping the path, a pebble flew and struck the bamboo, and when he heard the sound it made, he suddenly had a great satori. He bathed and purified himself and then went back to Ta-wei Mountain, where he burned incense and paid homage. Then he spoke to Ta-wei: "Ta-wei, Chief Priest, if you had answered me on that other occasion, how would this thing ever have been possible? The depths of your kindness exceed even those of my own parents." Then he composed this verse:

> With one blow of the pebble, everything I knew perished.
> What more is there for me to practice, what more to subdue?
> Moving about with ease, I conduct myself in the ancient Way,
> And I never feel any despondency.
> Wherever I am, I leave no traces;
> It is conduct apart from forms and sounds.
> Those in all the directions who are enlightened in the Way
> Are called "those of the highest talent."
> He presented this verse to Ta-wei, who said, "How thorough
> you are."

The Ch'an master Ling-yuan Chih-ch'in had practiced the Way for thirty years. Once, while wandering in the mountains, he paused at the foot of a hill and saw a place where people lived. It was spring, and when he saw the blossoms on a peach tree, he immediately became enlightened. He composed a verse and presented it to Ta-wei. It said,

> For thirty years I have sought the swordsman.
> How many times have the leaves fallen, or the branches broken off?

After once seeing the peach blossoms,
There is nothing more to doubt.

Ta-wei said, "The person who enters the Way according to circumstances never again regresses." In other words, Ta-wei acknowledged the enlightenment. Is there ever anyone who is not enlightened by circumstances? Does anyone ever slide back? I am not saying this only with regard to Chih-ch'in. Chih-ch'in finally became the Dharma heir of Ta-wei. If the forms of the mountains are not the pure body [of the Buddha], how could this happen?

A certain monk who was a disciple of Chang-sha Ching-ch'en asked his master, "How can I unite the mountains, streams, and great earth within myself?" The master replied, "How can you unite yourself with the mountains, streams, and great earth?" What is meant here is that if you are not anything other than your true self, then whether you speak of yourself being united with the mountains, streams, and great earth, [or of the mountains, streams, and great earth being united with yourself], there should not be any obstacles between what unites and that with which one is united.

Huang-chao, who was also known as the great master Hui-chüeh of Lang-yeh Mountain, was a distant descendant of Nan-yüeh's Dharma. Once, Tzu-hsüan, who gave lectures on the scriptures, asked him, "How does our pure, original nature instantly become mountains, streams, and the great earth?" Hui-chao tried to instruct him by asking him in turn, "How does our pure, original nature instantly give birth to the mountains, streams, and the great earth?" You must understand with regard to this that you should not mistakenly think that the original, pure nature as mountains, rivers, and the great earth, is the natural world of mountains, rivers, and the great earth. The person who just fumbles around in the sutras and has never heard this until now does not understand that the mountains, rivers, and the great earth are mountains, rivers, and the great earth. You must understand that if the pure nature, your original face, is not the forms of the mountains and the sounds of the valley streams, then the expounding of the Dharma by holding up a flower did not occur, nor did the acquiring of the marrow [of Bodhidharma] by Hui-k'o. Because of the merits of the forms of the mountains and sounds of the streams, the world and all sentient beings in it become enlightened at the same time, and like the Buddha himself, see the morning star and become all the Buddhas.

These sentient beings I have been speaking of were superior people whose spirit in seeking the Dharma was extremely profound. We of the present time ought to use their acts as models for our own efforts. In the present time, also, true followers of the Way should arouse such a spirit without regard for fame and fortune. In this time and place, so far from the land of Shakyamuni, true seekers of the Way are rare indeed. They are not non-existent, but one does not encounter them often. Even though they take their home departure and seem to be divorced from worldly ways, they are just using the Way in order to acquire fame and fortune. It is shameful, deplorable, that they traffic in evil karma because they have ignored time. Sometime, they may abandon [their wickedness] and acquire the Way. For the time being, they do not love the true dragon, even though they may meet a true teacher. Shakyamuni referred to such fellows as pitiful examples of humanity. Such fellows have reached this end because of the evil karma of previous lives. Because they lack the spirit to seek the Dharma for the sake of the Dharma, when they do meet the true dragon, they doubt whether they are seeing the real dragon, and are destroyed by it. Because their mind and body, their bone and flesh, have never been born in accordance with the Dharma, they consequently are not fit for the Dharma, and they cannot accept it. This Way has been transmitted from master to disciple over and over in this manner down to the present time.

Nowadays the mind that seeks satori is considered to be merely an ancient dream. How pitiful it is that, although you are born on the mountain of jewels, you do not know of these jewels or see them. How will you ever acquire the Dharma treasure? If you arouse the thought of seeking enlightenment, then afterward, even if you are born among the six destinations or in one of the four manners, the cause of your rebirth will be the practices and vows you made for the sake of satori. Thus, as it is said that just as the days and months of former times are all eternally past and gone, but one's present life is not yet over, so should one quickly make a vow. This vow is as follows: "I vow that I and all living beings in all lives from now on shall be able to hear the true Dharma, and when we hear it, we will be unable to doubt it, and it will be impossible not to have faith in it. When we come in contact with the true Dharma, we will abandon worldly ways and receive and accept the true Dharma. Later, the great earth and all sentient beings will achieve perfect Buddhahood. If you make a vow in this way, that will be the proper condition for arousing the thought of enlightenment. Do not be negligent in this.

Also, Japan is very far from foreign lands, and people here are extremely deluded. From ancient times until now, no saintly people have been born here, nor have there been any naturally intelligent people. Need I say that there have been no true followers of the Buddha's Way. When those who are ignorant of the mind that seeks the Way try to understand it, good advice hurts their ears, and even as they resent others, they do not reflect upon themselves.

Now with regard to your practice and vows, whether or not you have aroused the thought of enlightenment, whether or not you are practicing, do not let others know about it. Practice in such a way that it is not known. Never speak of it yourself. People today do not truly seek the Way, so they do not practice with their bodies or enlighten their minds, but still they are praised by others and sought out as individuals in whom practice and enlightenment have been fulfilled. This is nothing but delusion within delusion, and this kind of confused thinking should cease.

The difficulty of hearing the Dharma and seeing the truth easily when one is seeking the Way is the labor of one's heart's desire in the search for the true teaching. This labor of one's heart's desire has been transmitted from ancestor to ancestor as the brilliant light of the Buddha and as the mind of the Buddha. From the days when the Tathāgata dwelt in the world up to now there have always been those who were very concerned about fame and fortune in the practice of the Way. When they came in contact with the teaching of a true master and they had a change of heart and began to really seek the Dharma, then they naturally acquired the Way.

Now, when you practice the Way, you should know that certain problems may arise. For instance, you may be one of those with a "beginner's mind" who arouses the first thought of enlightenment, or one of those whose practice is mature, or you may have the opportunity to give the teaching to others and transmit the Way, or you may not have the opportunity. You may be able to develop a fondness for the teaching of the ancient Buddha and learn it, or you may be deprived of it and simply become a demon who does not learn it. But whichever it may be, do not become attached to either or be distressed about either. However, people of today are really unconcerned about this, which is merely indifference to either attachment or distress. The reason they do not worry about it is that they do not know about the three root poisons [of desire, hatred, and ignorance]. You should never forget the determination you had at the time you first aroused a joyous feeling about the Buddha Way and began seeking it. That is, when you arouse the thought of enlightenment, you should seek the Dharma for the sake of others, and reject fame and fortune. Do not desire fame and fortune, but just desire to obtain the Way at once. Consequently, do not expect to have the respect of the nation's ruler and his retainers, and do not expect to be honored by them. Even though such a situation has occurred in the past in which a monk received respect and honor from the ruler and his retainers, that person did not want it and did not seek it. Thus, in seeking the Way, you should hope that you will not become restricted by the respect and honor of men and gods.

However, the foolish people of the world, even though they have the mind that seeks the Way, lose their original determination quickly and mistakenly hanker after the honor of men and gods, pleased in their belief that they have gone as far as one can go in the Dharma. When the ruler and his retainers become eager to take refuge, these people think to themselves, "My Dharma has flowered to its fullest." This is one of the demons that appears when you undertake the Way. You should never neglect compassion for the ruler and his retainers, but you should not be delighted about it.

O monks, observe: the wise admonish us that even in the time of the Buddha there were, to quote the golden words of the Buddha, "many who slandered the Dharma even while following it." Thus, they damaged it. Ignorant people do not understand the precious nature of the Buddha Way, so they harm it. Nevertheless, these small, animal-like people are often considered to be among the assemblies of the wise. We also read that many of the Indian ancestors were injured by nonbelievers, followers of the small vehicle, and rulers. It is not because the nonbelievers were superior people, or that those injured were lacking in the knowledge of all Buddhas. When Bodhidharma came to China from India and stayed at Shaolin Monastery, not even the Emperor Wu knew about him, nor did the Emperor of Wei.

At that time, however, there were two dogs, Bodhiruci and Hui-kuang the Vinaya master, who were experts in the scriptures. Their own reputations being false, they feared true followers of the Way, knowing that their own teachings would be obscured like the sun behind the clouds, and so they tried to slander the true teachings. These two were feared by true followers of the Way even more than Devadatta, who lived at the time of the Buddha. It is sad, but the fame and fortune they so ardently sought was hated by Bodhidharma even more than the defilement of excrement. This situation, however, is not the result of any deficiency in the Dharma, and there have always been dogs who howled at good men. Don't be disturbed by the howling dogs, and do not bear a grudge against them. Instead, vow to guide them, in accordance with the passage [in the *Brahmajāla Sutra*] that says, "Even though you are dogs, you should arouse the thought of enlightenment." Our predecessors said with regard to this, "They are just animals with human faces."[40] There are also among the human-faced animals some demons who take refuge in the Buddha and honor him. The Buddha said, "You should not associate with rulers, princes, retainers, high dignitaries, Brahmins, or laymen."[41] Truly, this method of practice should not be forgotten by any of you who wish to learn the Buddha's Way. In this manner, in the individual who is just beginning to seek the Way for the first time as a bodhisattva, merits will accumulate as he progresses.

Also, since ancient times, the great god Shakra has appeared on earth to test the spirit of the seeker of the Way, or else Mara has appeared to disturb his practices. This happens when the follower of the Way does not give up his yearning for fame and fortune. When great compassion and great wisdom are deep, and one makes the vow to deliver all beings to the other shore of enlightenment, then there are no obstacles in one's path. The power of one's own practice is enough to win the ruler to the Way, and you may also see this as one of the blessings of worldly life. At such a time, you must penetrate to the truth and not be blind. The ignorant will take great delight, like foolish dogs gnawing on a dry bone. The wise will avoid this, just as ordinary people are revolted by excrement.

The person who has just aroused the thought of seeking the Way cannot fathom the Buddha Way by means of plotting and scheming. No matter how much he schemes, he never hits the mark. But even though he cannot enter the Way by plotting and scheming, this does not mean that he cannot attain the ultimate. The inner depths of attainment are not at all shallow in the same way that plotting and scheming are in the beginner. Therefore, you must just begin directly to train in the Way in the manner of those who have previously attained supreme *bodhi*. This means that you may have to climb the peaks of mountains and sail the deep oceans in order to visit a teacher and ask about the Way. If you call upon a teacher or solicit the help of a good friend, they descend from the heavens and appear out of the earth. As for the guidance of the true teacher, it is to be requested of sentient beings and even of insentient beings. Those who hear the teaching may hear it with their bodies or they may hear it with their minds. Hearing with one's ears is the usual way to do it, but hearing with one's eyes is also a way to penetrate to the truth. In seeing the Buddha, also, one may see one's own Buddha or the Buddha of others, one may see large Buddhas or small Buddhas. Don't be alarmed at seeing a large Buddha, and do not be troubled at seeing a small Buddha. Just recognize the so-called large Buddha or small Buddha as the forms of the mountains and the sounds of the valley streams. Here is the long, broad tongue of the Buddha, here are the myriad verses of the sutras that teach the Dharma. Here is the unobstructed, sovereign teaching of the Dharma, and here abides the one realm of satori.

dly beings may say, "When we look about, everything is
erything is broad." The Ch'an master Ju-ching said, "It is
lly empty, it is universally overflowing." It is nothing more
green of pines in the spring and the glory of chrysanthe-
autumn. When the good friend has reached the ground of

satori, he becomes a great teacher of men and gods. While he has still not reached this ground but recklessly tries to show the Way, he is nothing more than a big robber who harms men and gods. What faith has he who does not know the true body that is the spring pine, or the true reality that is, just as it is, the autumn chrysanthemum? How can he ever cut off the roots of birth and death?

Moreover, the mind and body are lazy, and if you lack faith, you should show a sincere heart and make repentance before the Buddhas and ancestors. If you do this, the power of the merit of repentance before the Buddhas will help and purify you. These merits create and sustain a pure faith and diligence that cannot be obstructed. Once this pure faith becomes evident, you yourselves and all others will be converted to the Buddha Way, and its benefits will extend everywhere to both sentient and insentient beings.

This is what you should do to repent: Say, "I ask that even though my past bad karma has greatly accumulated in me and is a cause for the obstruction of the Way, all the Buddhas and ancestors who have acquired the Way by means of the Buddha Way compassionately think of me and free me from my accumulated bad karma, and eliminate all the obstacles to my learning the Way. The merits of their Dharma teachings fill up the unbounded universe; may the Buddhas and ancestors extend their compassion to me. In the past, the Buddhas and ancestors were the same as we are now; in the future may we be the same as all Buddhas and ancestors." When we see all the Buddhas, all alike are one Buddha, one ancestor; when we think of putting forth the thought of enlightenment, we and all Buddhas likewise arouse the thought. With regard to extending compassion unlimitedly in all directions, sometimes we have the opportunity, and sometimes we do not. Thus, the Ch'an master Lung-ya said:

> Those in the past who were not enlightened will now be
>   enlightened;
> You ought to acquire this in this very life.
> When Buddhas were not enlightened, they were like
>   you are now;
> If you become enlightened now, you will be like the old Buddhas.

You should reflect deeply on this verse by Lung-ya. Be responsible for your own enlightenment. If you repent in this way, you will surely receive help from all the Buddhas, help that cannot be detected with your eyes. Concentrate your mind, arrange your body properly, kneel, and place your palms together in *gasshō,* and then repent all your past transgressions and evil acts before the Buddha. The power of repentance will destroy the roots of wickedness and make them vanish. This is the genuine, true practice; this is the mind that truly has faith, this is the body that truly has faith.

When you practice correctly, the sounds and forms of the valley streams and the forms and sounds of the mountains all become the myriad verses of the sutras. If you yourself do not prize fame and fortune or your own mind and body, and you are generous in abandoning them before the Buddhas and ancestors, then the valley streams and mountains will be generous in preaching the Dharma. Now, as for whether the streams and mountains reveal the myriad verses or not, it is beyond the power of the discriminating mind to know, but they are still the myriad verses, without doubt. If you yourself, who are the valley streams and mountains, cannot develop the power that illuminates the true reality of the mountains and valley streams, who else is going to be able to convince you that you and the streams and mountains are one and the same?

Hotsu Mujō Shin

"AROUSING THE SUPREME THOUGHT"

SHAKYAMUNI BUDDHA says [in the *Nirvana Sutra],* "The Himalaya Mountains are just like great nirvana." This is a very pertinent figure of speech. It is a simile that accurately grasps the Himalayas just as they are. The point that Shakyamuni made in making a simile of the Himalayas is that they are like nirvana in their exalted height. Both are identical in this respect.

However, Bodhidharma, the first Chinese ancestor, said, "The One Mind and all minds are wood and stone." What he calls "mind" is the absolute mind, the mind of the whole world, and so the One Mind is the mind of oneself and others. The minds of all the beings in the world, the minds of Buddhas and ancestors everywhere, and the minds of *devas* and *nagas* are wood and stone.[42] There is no mind apart from these. These stones and wood, or things in general, are not themselves bound by the realms of being and non-being, emptiness and form, and so on. One arouses the thought of enlightenment, practices, and attains with the mind that is wood and stone, because mind is wood and mind is stone. With the power of this mind that is wood and stone, the mind that is liberated now is manifested. Hearing and seeing the sounds and sights of the mind that is wood and stone, for the first time one transcends the views of those fellows outside the Dharma. There is no Buddhadharma apart from this.

Nan-yang Ta-cheng said, "The rubble filling in the wall is the mind of the ancient Buddhas." You should understand this by carefully studying what and where the stone and wood rubble are that are mind as stone and wood. "The mind of the ancient Buddhas" should not be understood as something irrelevant to your experience, as some mind that exists from the beginningless past, for it is the mind that eats rice gruel or tastes other food in your ordinary, everyday life; it is the mind that is grass, the mind that is water. Within this kind of life just as it is, it is the act of sitting like a Buddha and making an effort like a Buddha that is called "arousing the thought of enlightenment."

The conditions for arousing the thought of enlightenment do not come from anywhere else. It is the enlightened mind that arouses the thought of enlightenment. The meaning of this phrase, "it is the enlightened mind that arouses the thought of enlightenment" is that one makes a stupa with a blade of grass, one makes a sutra scroll with a rootless tree, one honors the Buddha with a grain of sand, one honors the Buddha with the water in which rice has been soaked, one offers a handful of food to living creatures, and one presents five flowers to the Tathāgata; this is arousing the thought of enlightenment. Following the encouragement of others, practicing good to even the slightest extent possible for you, bowing to the Buddha while you are being disturbed by demons, all these are also the arousing of the thought of enlightenment. Not only that, but knowing that one's home is not really one's home, abandoning home and going away from home, entering the mountains and practicing the Buddha's Way, practicing with faith or practicing according to the Dharma is also arousing the thought of enlightenment. It is making the image of a Buddha, making a stupa, reading the sutras, being mindful of the Buddha, preaching the Dharma for living beings, visiting a true teacher and asking questions, and sitting cross-legged and doing zazen. It is also bowing to the Buddha, Dharma, and Sangha, and it is reciting the words, "I take refuge in the Buddha."

Such conditions as these myriad practices are all forms of arousing the thought of enlightenment. Arousing the thought of enlightenment is also acquiring the Way when putting forth the thought of enlightenment within a dream, or acquiring the Way when putting forth the thought while drunk.[43] Or else it is acquiring the Buddha Way by putting forth the thought when one sees the spring flowers scattered by the wind, or when one sees the autumn leaves falling.[44] Or else it is acquiring the Way by putting forth the thought while seeing peach blossoms, or hearing a pebble strike green bamboo.[45] Or else it is acquiring the Way by putting forth the thought in the heavens or within the deep sea.[46] All these are examples of putting forth the thought of enlightenment within the thought of enlightenment. Putting forth the thought of enlightenment by means of the thought of enlightenment means putting forth the thought of enlightenment with one's own mind and body that are the mind of rivers and mountains. It is putting forth the thought of enlightenment within the minds and bodies of all the Buddhas. It is putting forth the thought of enlightenment within the skin, flesh, bones, and marrow of all the Buddhas and ancestors.

This being so, the making of Buddha images and stupas at this time are surely the arousing of the thought of enlightenment. Directly achieving perfect Buddhahood is surely the arousing of the thought of enlightenment. But do not stop just halfway, [thinking that you can do such things as read sutras, think of the Buddha, make stupas, and so on, merely formally]. Such things must be unconditioned merits,[47] the merits of non-self-assertive action.[48] Arousing the thought of enlightenment means having a correct understanding in accordance with the truth, or having a correct understanding in accordance with the nature of the Dharma. It is samādhi that gathers together [the merits] of all the Buddhas. It is the realization of the *dharani's* of all the Buddhas. It is the mind of unsurpassed, complete, perfect enlightenment. It is the fruit of arhatship. It is the manifestation of the Buddha. Outside of this arousing of the thought of enlightenment, there is no Buddha-dharma such as the unconditioned and so on.

In spite of this, the deluded followers of the small vehicle say, "Making Buddha images and erecting stupas are deeds done as mundane merit, so you should leave them alone and not do them. Stopping the discriminating mind and achieving one-pointedness of mind are unconditioned. The mind that neither arises nor ce[...] nothing. This is reality. The close inspection of the true [...] the nature of dharmas is satori." Both in India and China, i[...] times and now, it has been a common custom to claim th[...]

thing. Using this as a pretext, even though these people commit offenses against the precepts and are guilty of the five unpardonable acts, still they do not make Buddha images or erect stupas. Living in a world of passions as countless as the trees of a forest, dirtying themselves in muddy water as they do, they do not think of the Buddha nor do they read the sutras. They not only damage the Buddha seed of those who live in this world, but they even deny the very Buddha nature of the Tathāgata.

Truly this is regrettable. Even though they have been fortunate enough to meet the Buddha, Dharma, and Sangha, they still have become the bitter enemies of the Three Jewels. While they climb the mountain of the Three Jewels, they return with empty hands, and though they enter the ocean of the Three Jewels, they return with empty hands. Because of the existence of this state of affairs, even though a million Buddhas and ancestors are revealed in the world, these fellows never find the opportunity to come into contact with the Buddha Way, and they lose their grasp on the bodhi mind. The reason is that they do not follow the sutras, nor do they follow the advice of a good friend who wishes to help them. Rather, they follow false teachers who are outside the Way. The false view that making Buddha images and erecting stupas is not the same as arousing the thought of enlightenment should be abandoned at once. Do not pay any attention to false teachings and views about washing the mind, washing the body, washing the ears, or washing the eyes. At once be in accord with the Buddha's scriptures, follow a true teacher, take refuge in the true Buddhadharma, and learn and practice the Buddhadharma.

In the great Way of the Buddhadharma, all the sutra chapters in the universe are contained within a dust mote. Within a dust mote, an incalculable number of Buddhas dwell. A blade of grass or a leaf are the mind and body. If the myriad forms do not rise, neither does the One Mind rise. If all things are the revelation of ultimate reality, then a single dust mote is the revelation of ultimate reality. Therefore, the One Mind is all things, all things are the One Mind, they are the total body. If such things as making stupas is a conditioned effort, then enlightenment, that is to say Buddha result, and Buddha nature itself must be conditioned also. However, because

Buddha nature is not conditioned, neither is making Buddha images or erecting a stupa a conditioned act. They are the non-self-assertive acts of arousing the thought of enlightenment, and their merits are unconditioned and pure. Truly, they must be experienced, believed, and understood as the arousing of the thought of enlightenment. The eternal practice of the Way and the vow to emancipate all living beings are based on this arousing of the thought of enlightenment and are born from it. This arousing of the thought of enlightenment does not ever decay. This is called seeing the Buddha and hearing the Dharma.

You should understand that gathering together wood and stone, piling up mud and clay, and collecting gold, silver, and the seven precious stones and making a Buddha image or stupa is the same as making images and stupas by collecting together the One Mind. It is gathering together emptiness upon emptiness and making a Buddha. It is using mind upon mind and creating a Buddha. It is piling stupa upon stupa to make a stupa. It is manifesting Buddha upon Buddha to make Buddha. Consequently, the "Skillful Means" chapter of the *Lotus Sutra* says, "When you have this thought, all the Buddhas in the universe are revealed." You should understand that thinking just once of becoming a Buddha is the revelation of all the Buddhas in the universe. When one thing becomes a Buddha, all things become Buddhas. When Shakyamuni attained enlightenment, he said, "When the morning star appeared, I and the great earth with all its beings simultaneously became Buddhas." Therefore, arousing the thought of enlightenment, practice, bodhi, and nirvana are all simultaneous with the enlightenment, practice, bodhi, and nirvana of Shakyamuni. What we call the body and mind in the Buddha Way is grass, trees, and wall rubble; it is wind, rain, water, and fire. When you reflect on these things and cause the development of the Buddha Way, it is arousing the thought of enlightenment. Using space to make an image of the Buddha or to erect a stupa is arousing the thought of enlightenment. Scooping up the valley streams is making a Buddha image or stupa. It is the arousal of *anuttara samyak sambodhi*. It is a myriad arousings of one thought of enlightenment. The same is true with regard to practice and attainment.

However, if your understanding is that arousing the thought of enlightenment is just a single arousing of the thought of enlightenment and that there are no other arousings, and that while practices are numerous, attainment is a single attainment, you do not really understand the Buddhadharma, nor can you grasp it, nor can you come into contact with it. Myriad arousings of the thought of enlightenment are surely one arousing; the arousing of the thought of enlightenment by myriad people is the arousing of the thought by a single person. The arousing of the thought of enlightenment by a single person is the arousing of the thought by myriad people. The same is true of practice, attainment, and the turning of the wheel of the Dharma. If your own body and mind are not grass, wood, and so on, then they are not your body and mind. And if your own body and mind do not exist, neither do grass and wood. If grass and wood do not exist, then they are not grass and wood.

The practice of zazen and learning the Way are the arousal of the thought of enlightenment. Arousing the thought of enlightenment is neither identical with zazen nor different from it, and zazen is neither the same as the arousal of the thought of enlightenment nor different from it, nor are they two things, nor are they three, nor are they different. You should study everything in the same way.

From beginning to end, when you collect grass and wood and the seven precious stones and use them to make a Buddha image or stupa, if you feel that you cannot achieve the Buddha Way because these are conditioned acts, then the thirty-seven parts of enlightenment are also conditioned. Practicing the Way with the mind and body of a human being or god is also conditioned. If this is the case, you will not achieve the ultimate stage.

Grass, wood, wall rubble, the four elements, and the five *skandhas* are all identical in being nothing but Mind; all alike have the true mark.[49] All the worlds in the ten directions are ultimate reality, Buddha nature; all are identically Dharma abode, Dharma state.[50] Within ultimate reality and Buddha nature there is no grass, wood, or wall rubble; within grass, wood, and wall rubble, there is no ultimate reality or Buddha nature. Dharmas are not mundane and conditioned, nor are they supramundane and unconditioned; they are the manifestation of ultimate reality, they are just what they are in themselves. Things being just what they are in themselves are *thus—*

absolute reality. This *thus* is your present body and mind. It is within this body and mind that you should arouse the thought of enlightenment. Do not dislike treading on water or stone.[51] Just use a blade of grass to make a six-foot golden Buddha body, or use a speck of dust to build a stupa to the ancient Buddhas, and this itself is arousing the thought of enlightenment. It is seeing the Buddha and it is hearing the Buddha. It is seeing the Dharma and hearing the Dharma. It is becoming a Buddha and acting like a Buddha.

Shakyamuni Buddha said, "The upāsaka and the upāsika and the sons and daughters of good family honor the Three Jewels with the flesh of their wives and children, and they honor the Three Jewels with their own flesh. After monks have received these alms of faith, they surely must practice." This being so, what you must understand is that honoring the Three Jewels with food, clothing, bedding, medicine, monasteries, fields, and woodlands is to do honor with one's own body, as well as the flesh, skin, bone, and marrow of one's spouse and children. When these merge with the ocean of merits of the Three Jewels, all become one. When they become one, they are the Three Jewels. The merits of the Three Jewels becoming a reality in your own body and in the skin, flesh, bones and marrow of your spouse and children is the earnest and vigorous effort of learning the Way. Considering the World-honored One's nature and teachings to be your own nature and teachings means considering the skin of the Buddha Way to be your own skin; it means considering the flesh of the Buddha Way to be your own flesh; it means considering the bones of the Buddha Way to be your own bones; it means considering the marrow of the Buddha Way to be your own marrow. What is called alms of faith is the arousing of the thought of enlightenment, and the monk who receives it should practice. The giver must be a true giver, and the recipient must be a true recipient.

When the thought of enlightenment, which may be no bigger than a speck of dust, is aroused, the One Mind is aroused with it. When the One Mind is aroused for the first time, the one emptiness is also aroused in that instant. When all Buddhas and ordinary beings have aroused the thought of enlightenment, then for the f̄ time the one Buddha nature that has existed all along in seed fo is realized. When you use the total power of the four elements and five skandhas and practice earnestly, you will acquire the Way. This is because the four elements and five skandhas, grass, wood, and wall rubble, are all identically involved in practice, and because all are identical in their nature. They have the same mind, the same life, the same body, and the same activity.

There have been many disciples of the Buddha ancestors who learned the Way by making the mind of grass and wood their own mind. This is the sign of the arousing of the thought of enlightenment. The fifth ancestor was once employed as a tree planter. Lin-chi made his practice the planting of cedar and pine when he was at Mount Huang-po. There is the story of an old man by the name of Lo, who was a contemporary of Tung-shan Wu-pen, who also planted pines. All gouged out the eyes of the Buddha ancestors [and made them their own] using the high moral principles of pine and oak. This is fervently practicing the Way by practically utilizing the ability to make the eyes of the Buddhas and ancestors your own. Making Buddha images and stupas and so on are all ways of using their eyes. It is tasting the arousal of the thought of enlightenment. It is using the arousal of the thought of enlightenment. Therefore, those who cannot acquire the eyes of stupa building and Buddha making cannot achieve the Way of the Buddhas and ancestors. As soon as you acquire the eyes that consist of making a Buddha image, you become a Buddha, you become a ancestor.

Some say, "The Buddha images and stupas later turn back to earth again, and so the merit of making them cannot be real, but training is like durable metal that does not turn back to earth," but this is not the teaching of the Buddha. If it is claimed that the stupa that has been erected is changed back to earth again, the unproduced also returns to earth again. If the unproduced does not return to earth again, neither does the stupa become earth again. According to the Buddhas and ancestors, "Within these [activities] is the abiding place of *this*. It is called nirvana and samsara."

According to a sutra, "When a bodhisattva confronting samsara first arouses the thought of enlightenment and earnestly seeks bodhi, he becomes firm and unshakeable. The merits of this one thought are deep, extensive, boundless. If the Tathāgata were to discuss and distinguish them for many eons, he could not exhaust their number." You should clearly understand that using samsara to arouse the thought of enlightenment is the same as earnestly seeking bodhi. His one thought is identical with a single blade of grass or a tree, because it is one life and one death.

However, the depths of these merits are limitless, and they are boundless in breadth. Their number cannot be exhausted even though the Tathāgata discusses and distinguishes them for many eons. Even though the ocean may be dried up, its bottom remains, and even though a man dies, his mind remains, so it cannot be exhausted either. And just as this one thought is deep, broad, and boundless, so is a blade of grass, a tree, a stone, or a tile also boundless in depth and breadth. If the grass or stone is seven or eight feet high, then so is this one thought seven or eight feet high.

This being so, entering the deep mountains and thinking about the Buddha Way is comparatively easy, while building stupas and making Buddha images [which are the arousing of the thought of enlightenment] is very difficult. Although both are achieved through energy and the lack of neglect and laziness, using mind and having one's mind and body used by mind are very different. Arousing the thought of enlightenment in such a way goes on manifesting Buddha ancestors eternally.

Shukke

"HOME DEPARTURE"

THE *Ch'an yüan ch'ing kuei*[52] says, "All the Buddhas of the past, future, and present have taught home departure and achievement of the Way. All the twenty-eight Indian ancestors and the six Chinese ancestors who have transmitted the seal of the Buddha mind were *shramanas*. All who left the home life were afterward able to become the teachers of the three worlds because they upheld the moral precepts *(shīla)* of the Buddha Way. Consequently, when you practice Zen and seek the true teacher, you should give priority to the observance of these precepts. If you do not free yourselves from worldly delusion and dissociate yourselves from evil acts by upholding the pure precepts of the Buddha Way, there is no way for you to ever become a Buddha or ancestral teacher. You must receive the precepts *[jukai]*."

"In order to receive the precepts of home departure, you must supply yourselves with the three robes, bowl, eating utensils, cushion, and new underclothes. If you do not have new underclothes, you may use some that have been washed, but when you enter the place where you are going to receive the precepts, you must not use someone else's robes and bowl. Concentrate single-mindedly on the Buddha Way, be modest in mind and body, model yourself on the Buddha, unite the precepts to your own mind and body, and make the Buddha mind your own mind. This is very important in the life of home departure, so do not neglect it. If you just borrow robes and bowl and go where the precepts are given, it will be as if you had not received them. If you do not receive the precepts by following these regulations, you are probably the kind of person who will not be able to receive the precepts in this life. By entering the Dharma gate carelessly, you become the kind of person who receives the offering of the faithful in vain. When you are introduced to the Way for the first time and still do not understand the precepts, then if your teacher does not teach them to you, he is leading you down the wrong path. Therefore, I am now giving you this frank advice. I hope very much that you will engrave it on your hearts and never forget it. If you receive the precepts of the *Shrāvakas* of the small vehicle, you should next be diligent about receiving the bodhisattva precepts, because this is the proper sequence of entering the door of the Dharma."

Clearly understand that the achievement of the Way by all the Buddhas and ancestors was only through home departure and receiving the precepts. The life pulse of the Buddhas and ancestors is only home departure and receiving the precepts. If you still have not made your home departure, neither are you a Buddha ancestor. Seeing the Buddha, seeing the patriarchs, is making your home departure and receiving the precepts.

Mahākāshyapa[53] left the home life to follow the Buddha in his wish to be freed of all defilements. The Buddha said to him, "Welcome, monk," and his hair and beard spontaneously fell to the ground and his body was spontaneously covered with monks' robes. It is clear from the traces we have of all the Buddhas that all who practiced the Way and freed themselves from defilements have made their home departure and received the precepts.

According to the third volume of the *Large Sutra on the Perfection of Wisdom,*[54] the Buddha, the World-Honored One, said, "If a bodhisattva, a great being, thinks, 'Someday I will surely abandon the ranks of the court and leave the home life, and on that day I will attain supreme bodhi. Also, on that day, when I leave the home life, I will turn the wonderful wheel of the Dharma and cause countless, numberless beings to abandon wickedness and delusion and produce the pure Dharma vision. Then I will cause them to exterminate their impurities forever and become wise and emancipated. Moreover, I will cause them to become irreversible in supreme bodhi,' then this bodhisattva who desires to accomplish such a thing should extensively study the *Perfection of Wisdom.*"

Supreme enlightenment is acquired on the day one leaves the home life and receives the precepts. If there is no day of home departure, there is no day of supreme enlightenment. Thus, the dawning of the day of your home departure is the dawning of the day when you achieve supreme enlightenment, and the dawning of the day when you achieve supreme enlightenment is the dawning of the day of your home departure. This is the day when your layman's body, just as it is, is transformed into a Buddha's body, and you attain supreme enlightenment and preach the Dharma for the sake of all beings. Your home departure itself causes many living beings to enter the Buddha Way. It is the practice of self-benefit and benefit to others that causes them to experience supreme enlightenment and acquire irreversibility.

You should understand that when you have perfected this self-benefit and benefit to others, this is itself the seeking of supreme enlightenment and becoming irreversible, and this immovability is nothing other than leaving the home life and receiving the precepts. Attaining supreme enlightenment enlightens us to the fact that the day of home departure is the day of supreme enlightenment. What you should understand correctly is that the day of home departure is the day when the opposition between enlightenment and the first thought of enlightenment is transcended. This absolute time is the time of liberation. The day of home departure is the day when you know from inner experience that the time of three incalculable eons is the eternal now of the day of home departure. This day of home departure contains within itself the time when you dwell in the boundless oceans of the eons and teach the Dharma to all beings. The time of home departure is not a small period of time, such as that required for eating a meal, nor is it the unthinkable time of sixty small eons; it is time that transcends time. It is time that freed the Buddha's topknot. The day of home departure even transcends the day of home departure. The day of home departure is truly the day of home departure when you have overcome attachment and reached the state of dropping off mind and body. The day of achieving the Way is the day of achieving the Way; that is, the day of home departure is the day when you achieve the Way, and the day when you achieve the Way is the day of home departure.

The following is recorded in the thirteenth volume of the *Ta chih tu lun:* "When the Blessed One was staying in the Jetavana Grove, a drunken Brahmin came to the Buddha and said that he wanted to leave the home life. At this, the Buddha had some monks shave off the Brahmin's hair and dress him in the robes of a monk. The Brahmin sobered up and was surprised to discover his altered appearance, and he left. Some monks then asked the Buddha why he had allowed the Brahmin to leave the home life. The Buddha replied, 'Never in all the ages up to now has that Brahmin ever thought of home departure. Now while he was drunk, it was a small matter for him to think that he wanted to leave the home life, but because this happened, in a later time he will really leave the home life.'"[55] Thus, there are various conditions for home departure. It is better to break the precepts as one who has left the home life than to observe them as a householder, because a householder cannot be liberated by the precepts.

You should understand the truth of the Buddha's words. The fundamental requirement of the Way is home departure. He who has not yet left the home life cannot acquire the Buddhadharma. When the Buddha was still in the world, various nonbelievers had already given up their wicked ways through their own faith, but when they took refuge in the Buddhadharma, they necessarily asked for home departure and the precepts.

Sometimes the Blessed One himself says in a friendly manner, "Welcome, monk," and thereby acknowledges home departure, and sometimes he gathers monks about him and has them shave their hair and beards and thus leave the home life and receive the precepts. In both cases, the Dharma of home departure and receiving the precepts is fulfilled in the minds and bodies of these people. You should understand how great are the merits of home departure and receiving the precepts. When the Buddha's efforts flood the minds and bodies of these people, their hair falls spontaneously to the ground and the *kesa* covers their bodies. If the Buddha does not acknowledge home departure, their hair is not shaved and the kesa does not cover their bodies. This means that the person has not yet received the Buddha's precepts. This being so, home departure and receiving the precepts is the new prediction of all Buddha Tathāgatas that Buddhahood is certain.

Shakyamuni Buddha said, "Sons of good family, the Tathāgata perceives that those who practice the Dharma in the small vehicle are slight of merit and laden with impurities, and it is for their sake that I left the home life and attained supreme enlightenment when I was young. However, in truth, my experience of enlightenment really occurred many, many ages ago. Now, in the present time, I exercise skillful means in order to educate beings and cause them to enter the Dharma, and so I say this. Although I experienced enlightenment long, long ago, I say that I left the home life when young. 'I attained supreme enlightenment' means 'I made my home departure when young.' When I departed the home life when young, beings who followed the small vehicle and whose merits were few and whose impurities were many left the home life with me when I was young. When I experienced the Dharma teaching of 'home departure when I was young,' I experienced the Buddha's enlightenment. So, in order to aid beings who delight in the Dharma of the small vehicle, I say that I left the home life when young and experienced supreme enlightenment." This may be so, but it still may be asked what the merits of home departure are. The answer is that the merits of home departure are countless and unlimited.

Raihai Tokuzui

"PAYING HOMAGE AND
ACQUIRING THE ESSENCE"

WHEN ONE IS INVOLVED in the cultivation of *anuttara samyak sambodhi,* it is most difficult to find the proper master. This master has nothing at all to do with such characteristics as male and female and so on, but the teacher must be one who is intimately acquainted with *satori,* one who is of the highest rank. The teacher is neither a young person nor an old person, and even if the teacher is the apparition of a wild fox, he will be a good teacher. The teacher has the appearance of one who has acquired the marrow of the Dharma,[56] and he will guide and benefit beings. He is one who does not disregard the law of cause and effect. He may be "you," "me," or "her" for the true teacher is completely empty.

As soon as a person meets a true teacher, he should cast off all the myriad conditions and, without wasting a second, vigorously study the Way. He should do zazen and learn the Way whether with no thought, with thought, or with half-thoughts. But in any case, he should practice single-mindedly, like one trying to extinguish a blaze in his hair, or like one standing on one foot. Acting in this way, he will not be troubled by demons who slander the Dharma. He is none other than the second ancestor, who cut off his own arm in order to acquire the essence. He himself is none other than the teacher who has cast off mind and body.

Acquiring the essence of the Dharma and transmitting it necessarily depends on sincerity and faith. Sincerity and faith are not things that come from outside or inside; they are only acquired by valuing the Dharma and transforming oneself completely. They are acquired by renouncing the world and making the Way one's real home. If one thinks even a little of his own body, and values it more than the Dharma, he will not acquire the Way nor will he transmit it. The spirit that values the Way is not one or two, but even though we do not expect to get the teaching of another, let us provisionally accept it as one or two. That is to say, if the mind treasures the Dharma, then one's helper may be a pillar, a lantern, all the Buddhas, a fox, a demon, male or female, but if one protects and supports the great Dharma in his own body, if he has received the essence of all the Buddhas and ancestors, and if he has cast off mind and body, then even for countless eons he will devote his own mind and body to the practice of the Way. Acquiring a mind and body is fairly easy, just as rice, hemp, bamboo, and reeds exist in the world in great numbers, but it is rare to meet the Dharma.

Shakyamuni Buddha said, "When you meet a teacher who expounds the matter of supreme enlightenment, you should not think about his family lineage, pay attention to his appearance, pay any heed to his shortcomings, or criticize his actions. But because you value the wisdom of *prajñā*, you should feed him daily to the extent of a million *ryō* in gold. Pay homage to him with food fit for celestial beings. Three times daily you should pay homage and honor him, and never make him troubled in his mind. In this manner the Way of enlightenment will surely appear. Since I first put forth the thought of enlightenment up to now, I have practiced in this way, and I have acquired the highest enlightenment."

Therefore, you should entreat trees and rocks to preach the Dharma, and you should ask rice fields and gardens for the truth. Ask pillars for the Dharma, and learn from hedges and walls. Long ago the great god Indra honored a wild fox as his own master and sought the Dharma from him, calling him "Great Bodhisattva." It had nothing to do with whether the teacher was in a high or low form because of past karma.

However, deluded beings who have not heard the Buddha's Dharma think, "I am a high monk with much seniority and I cannot honor young monks even if they have acquired the Dharma. I have been engaged in practice for many years, and I cannot honor someone who has become a monk late in life, even if he has acquired the Dharma. I have been given the title of master, and I cannot honor someone who is not a master, even if he has acquired the Dharma. I am an important administrator in the clergy, and I cannot honor an ordinary monk, even if he has acquired the Dharma. I am a high priest, and I cannot honor laymen and laywomen, even if they have acquired the Dharma. I have reached a very high stage of the bodhisattva path, and I cannot honor nuns and others, even if they have acquired the Dharma. I am related by blood to the ruling family, and I cannot honor those who are not, even if they have acquired the Dharma." These foolish people abandon their fatherland and vainly tread the byways of foreign lands, and consequently they cannot see the Buddha's path.

Long ago during the T'ang Dynasty there was a great master named Chao-chou who had aroused the thought of enlightenment, and when he set out on a pilgrimage he made this vow: "Even if the person is only seven years old, if he is my superior, I shall seek the teaching from him. Even if he is a hundred years old, if he is inferior to me, I shall teach him." If a person seeks the Dharma from a seven-year-old, the older person should pay homage to him. Truly, this is the spirit of the great man. He is one who has the spirit of the ancient Buddhas. If a nun appears who has acquired the Way, who has acquired the Dharma, the monk who is seeking the Dharma should become her disciple, and asking her about the Dharma and paying homage to her is the mark of a person who excels in practicing the Buddha Way. It is like looking for drinking water when you are thirsty.

Zen master Chih-hsien was a great master who was a disciple of Lin-chi. When Lin-chi saw him coming to his place for the first time, he invited him to stay there, at which Chih-hsien accepted. Lin-chi said to him, "Stay with me for awhile as my disciple." Thus, Chih-hsien became his disciple. Later, he left Lin-chi and went to see a nun named Mo-shan. Mo-shan asked, "Where did you come from?" "I come from Lu-k'ou." (Literally, "I come from mouth-of-the road village.") Mo-shan replied, "Then why didn't you close it when you came here?" To this, Chih-hsien had no answer. He honored her with a bow and thus became her disciple. Later, he asked Mo-shan, "What is a summit mountain?" (Literally, *Mo-shan* means "summit mountain.") Mo-shan said, "It is the mountain summit that cannot be seen by a person because it is shrouded in clouds." Chih-hsien then asked, "Who is this person in the mountains?" Mo-shan said, "It has no male or female form; it transcends form." Again Chih-hsien posed a question, "[If it is neither male nor female, then if it is just the apparition of a fox,] why not change it into some other form?" Said Mo-shan, "Since it is not a fox apparition, I will not transform it into anything." Chih-hsien just bowed. Consequently, he aroused the thought of enlightenment, and stayed there to be supervisor of the fields for three years. Later, as chief priest of a monastery, he said to a group of monks, "When I was with the compassionate father Lin-chi, I got half a dipper full; at the compassionate mother Mo-shan's, I got the other half. Both halves united into the full Buddhadharma, and still today I am completely filled with the Dharma water of satori."

Now, reflecting on this story, Mo-shan was a prominent disciple of Kao-an Ta-yu. Her power of satori was superior, and she became the mother who taught Chih-hsien. Lin-chi had inherited the Dharma of the great Zen master Huang-po. His was the great power of practice, and he became the father of Chih-hsien. The father was male and the mother was female. Chih-hsien showed that he had a superior spirit when he sought the Dharma from Mo-shan and paid homage to her. He was unflagging in his pursuit of later training, and he is famous for seeking the Dharma without consideration of male and female.

Miao-hsin was a nun and the disciple of Hui-chi. One time, Hui-chi was about to select a monk to be chief in charge of external affairs, and he sought out some older monks, asking them, "I wonder who is most fit to become chief of external affairs?" After getting several suggestions, he said, "Even though Hsien-huai tzu [i.e., Miao-hsin] is a woman, she has the spirit of the superior person, and she is the most suitable for the position." All the monks there assented to this. Thus, Miao-hsin came to be chief in charge of external affairs. At that time, the advanced disciples of Hui-chi did not find this to be unsatisfactory. Even though this was not a very important position, we cannot overlook the fact that she was selected.

Later, when Miao-hsin was occupied as chief of external affairs, a party of seventeen monks from Szechwan who were visiting the great teachers of various areas came to Yang-shan to pay their respects, and they stayed in the guest house. While resting that night, they had a conversation concerning the famous *mondō* about the wind and the flag.[57] None of what the seventeen monks said really hit the mark. Miao-hsin, on the other side of the wall, heard what they said and made this comment: "Seventeen blind donkeys walk the road and without a bit of regret use up any number of straw sandals. But the Buddhadharma is never found in a dream." Some lay people who were with Miao-hsin heard her criticism and related it to the seventeen monks. None of them felt any resentment about being criticized by the chief of external affairs. They realized that they still had not acquired the Way, and at once they straightened their robes, lit incense and paid homage, and renewed their vows. Miao-hsin sent a request for them to appear before her. When they had gathered, she said to them, "It is not the wind that moves, it is not the flag that moves, and it is not the mind that moves." Having heard this, the seventeen monks were enlightened. They bowed and became her disciples. Then they directly departed from Yang-shan and returned west to Szechwan. Truly, such an example as this cannot be found among those in the higher stages of bodhisattva practice;[58] it was the act of those who have transmitted the Dharma directly from all the Buddhas and ancestors.

Therefore, when the chief priest of the monastery and his deputy are not around, you should look for a nun who has acquired the Way. Even if a monk is older and has been ordained for a long time, if he has not acquired the Dharma, do not try to use him. The person who is responsible for guiding those who are involved in practice must certainly be a person who has opened his Dharma eye. Ignorant people who are rigidly chained to external appearances and become objects of ridicule even from a worldly standpoint are indeed numerous. How much truer it is from the standpoint of the Dharma. There is no doubt that there are many who will not pay homage to women or nuns even if they have acquired the Dharma and transmitted it. They do not understand the Dharma, and since they do not study it, they are like animals, far removed from Buddhas and ancestors.

However, if you just earnestly abandon your own mind and body to the Buddhadharma with firm resolve, the Buddhadharma will surely reveal itself to you. Even among foolish humans and gods, hearts are moved by the truth, for how can the true Dharma of all the Buddhas not compassionately move the sincere heart? In earth, stones, sand, and pebbles, there is to be found the extremely inconceivable Mind that moves the sincere heart.

In the monasteries and temples of contemporary Sung China, there are places where nuns practice the Dharma, and if it is heard that a nun has acquired the Buddhadharma, the emperor issues an imperial edict making her the chief priest of a monastery. This means that she preaches the Dharma in the Dharma Hall of the monastery. The nuns who study under her congregate in the Dharma Hall, and while standing, conduct the ceremonies of the Dharma Hall and hear the Dharma preached. There is also an exchange of questions and answers *(mondō)*. This has been the custom since ancient times. In other words, one who has acquired the Dharma is a real ancient Buddha; there are no other ancient Buddhas to encounter. When the person in training meets me (and I have acquired the Dharma), he interviews me on the entirely new level of Buddha ancestor. When I, who have acquired the Dharma, meet a trainee, yesterday is forgotten, and I interview that person in the present that is only the present. For instance, when you make Dharma inquiries of a nun who transmits the treasury of the eye of the true dharma, who has reached the stage of arhat and *pratyeka-buddha*, who has reached the bodhisattva's last ten stages, and you pay homage to her, the nun will naturally receive your homage. What is there about a male intrinsically to esteem? The body is empty, like the sky; empty is empty, the four elements are the four elements, and the five aggregates are the five aggregates wherever they are found. The female is no different from a male, so both male and female acquire the Dharma without distinction. It is nothing more than taking seriously the experience of the Buddha Way. So do not think about such differences as male and female. This is the most basic law of the Buddha Way.

Also, in Sung China, practicing householders are persons who have not yet made their home departure and become a monk or nun. They live in a hermitage, and their spouse lives with them. Sometimes there are people who live celibate lives, and they are said to still be afflicted with delusion and turmoil. However, be that as it may, if they are truly involved in practice, honor their teacher, and search for the Dharma, they are no different from someone who has made his home departure. Even though one is a woman, even though one is an animal, it is the same. He who still does not see the truth of the Buddha Way, even if he is an aged monk a hundred years old, is not the equal of a man or woman who has acquired the Way. These old monks are not to be given the three bows of homage, although they are entitled to the courtesy due to a host or superior. But they are not to be given any special homage.

Even a seven-year-old girl who practices the Buddhadharma and is enlightened is the leader and guide of the fourfold community of Buddhists, the compassionate parent of living beings.[59] For instance, the naga-maiden in the *Lotus Sutra* achieved Buddhahood. Giving respect and homage to someone like her is the same as giving it to all the Buddhas. That is, it is the ancient etiquette of the Buddha Way. If you cannot understand this, you will regrettably be unable to transmit the Buddha Way.

There have been women who have ascended the throne in China and Japan both in ancient times and recently. These lands are possessions of the throne, so the inhabitants of these countries are the subjects of the ruler. The people respect the ruler not as a person but for the rank. It is the same with regard to nuns; from ancient times they have been respected not as people but because they have experienced the Buddha Way.

Nuns who reach the stage of arhat[60] acquire the merits of the four fruits[61] and they conform [mentally and physically] to these merits. There are few among humans or celestial beings whose merits exceed those of the four fruits. All fall short of these merits. Since these merits are lacking in humans and celestials, humans and celestials respect them. Who would not respect someone who has aroused the Buddha mind of the bodhisattva and transmits the true Dharma? Anyone who does not, slights himself, for he is himself the supreme enlightenment, and if he does not respect it, he is a fool who slanders the Dharma.

In Japan, the daughters of rulers and courtiers are like imperial consorts, hence, they have sometimes received royal titles. Some of these women have become nuns, while others have not. However, when monks who hanker for fame and fortune approach this kind of woman, they prostrate themselves at her feet and revere her. They are worse than servants of the ruler. How many of them will grow old as manservants of these women! It is sad that because they were born in a small country on the periphery of things they do not understand that this behavior is wrong. This does not happen in India or China but only in our own country.

Regrettably, by recklessly shaving off their hair while destroying the true Dharma, these monks incur a heavy karmic debt. By forgetting that the things of the world are like dreams and mirages, they end up as the servants of noblewomen, which is regrettable. Since they do these things for the sake of the vanities of the world, how will they ever come to honor and respect the experience of the eminently respectable Dharma for the sake of supreme awakening? Their determination to be serious about the Dharma is feeble because the determination to seek it is imperfect. When they covet valuables, they do not think that those valuables are unobtainable because a woman owns them. When they seek the Dharma, their determination must be even greater. If it is, then even grass, trees, and fences bestow the Dharma; heaven and earth and the myriad things provide it. This principle should be understood. Even if you have encountered a true teacher, if you have not yet aroused this determination and do not seek the Dharma, you will never be able to bathe in the pure water of the Dharma. You must make diligent effort.

Also, nowadays there are some extremely stupid men who think, "Women are nothing but sexual objects and providers of food." They neglect to consider that this kind of thinking results from wrong views. The Buddha's children should not be like this. If you detest women because they are objects of desire, shouldn't you also detest all men? When impure conditions occur, men become objects of desire, women become objects of desire, and those who are neither men nor women become objects of desire. Things in dreams and mirages become objects of desire. Or perhaps reflections in water give rise to impure conduct, or perhaps such conduct occurs as the result of the sun. Spirits become objects of desire, and demons do also. You cannot count all the conditions that produce desire, for it is said that there are eighty-four thousand of them. Aren't all these things to be abandoned? Aren't all of them to be ignored?

The precepts *(Vinaya)* say, "The three places of the female and two places of the male are alike completely forbidden." However, if people dislike objects of desire, then all men and women will dislike each other, and in that case they cannot hope for liberation. You must reflect upon this principle in minute detail. Even non-Buddhists may not have spouses, but still, if they do not become Buddhists, they hold wrong views. Among the Buddha's followers the two groups [of laymen and laywomen] have husbands or wives, but still, if they are followers of the Buddha, they do not attempt to equalize heaven and earth [by denying the law of cause and effect].

There are foolish monks in China who vow, "I shall not look at a woman for countless lives to come." What Dharma is this vow based on? Is it the Dharma of ordinary society? Is it the Buddha-dharma? A non-Buddhist Dharma? The Dharma of celestial beings or demons? What demerit is there in femaleness? What merit is there in maleness? There are bad men and good women. If you wish to hear the Dharma and put an end to pain and turmoil, forget about such things as male and female. As long as delusions have not yet been eliminated, neither men nor women have eliminated them; when they are all eliminated and true reality is experienced, there is no distinction of male and female. If you make a vow not to see a woman for ages and ages to come, won't you be neglecting them when you vow, "Sentient beings are numberless; I vow to save them"? If you neglect them, you are no bodhisattva. Is this the great compassion of the Buddha? This vow is the raving of a drunkard who has drunk deeply from the wine barrel of the small vehicle.[62] Neither humans nor celestial beings believe that this conforms to the true teaching.

Moreover, if you hate women because in past lives they violated the precepts, then since all bodhisattvas violated the precepts in past lives, shouldn't you hate them too? If you dislike women on the assumption that they will violate the precepts at some later time, then you must hate all bodhisattvas who have aroused the thought of enlightenment, because they too will violate the precepts in some future time. Hating in this manner, you consequently have abandoned everyone. Who will be responsible for manifesting the Buddhadharma in the world? Your vow is nothing but the crazy words of someone who does not understand the Buddhadharma. Pitiful! If you make such a vow, you should quietly consider whether all bodhisattvas starting with Shakyamuni have committed wrong acts and whether the thought of enlightenment they aroused is more shallow than your own.

None of the ancestral teachers who have been associated with the Dharma treasury, and none of the bodhisattvas who dwelt in the world in the Buddha's time, has ever made such a vow, and therefore you should examine carefully whether it is necessary for practicing and realizing the Buddhadharma. If you make this vow, not only will you not help to liberate women, but if a woman who has experienced the Dharma appears in the world, you will not go and question her when she teaches the Dharma for humans and celestial beings. If you do not go and question her, you are not a bodhisattva; in fact, you are not a Buddhist.

When we look at China, we see monks who seem to have refined their practice for a long time and who know every grain of sand in the ocean [of teachings] but who still flounder in the ocean of life and death. But there are women who visit a teacher, question him, do zazen, and become the teachers of humans and celestials. For instance, there was the old woman who would not sell rice cakes [to a monk] but threw them out instead.[63] It is pitiful, but there are male monks who know every item of doctrine in the scriptures and treatises but who do not see the Buddhadharma even in a dream. When you meet someone like this, consider deeply whether he can be enlightened. If you just avoid him as someone to be dreaded, this is the conduct of a disciple of the small vehicle. If you run from the east to take refuge in the west, you will find the same kind of person in the west. Even if you do run away and do not try to clear up his delusions, you will find such men near or far. What is more, to fail to liberate him and run away just deepens his delusion.

There is also something laughable to be found in Japan. There are restricted territories,[64] including Mahayana Buddhist training centers, which are prohibited to nuns and other women. This wrong custom has come down from the distant past and people do not realize that it is wrong. The custom is not changed by experts in legal matters nor is it studied by scholars. It is said to be either the practice of authorities in these matters or the custom of our predecessors, but it is never discussed, and if you laugh at it, it is like a stab in the vitals to others. Who are "authorities"? Are they wise or virtuous? Are they spirits or demons? Have they attained the stage of the ten virtues or the three wisdoms, or the stages of uniform enlightenment or wonderful enlightenment? And if you argue that past customs are not to be changed, does this mean that the endless turning on the wheel of birth and death [which results from past acts] is not to be changed?

Need I mention how perfectly enlightened our great teacher Shakyamuni was? He was enlightened in the way one ought to be enlightened, he practiced what ought to be practiced, and he achieved all the liberations in which one ought to be liberated. Can anyone today even begin to approximate him? Now, in the Buddhist community of his time, there were the four groups consisting of monks, nuns, laymen, and laywomen. There were also the eight groups [of beings outside the human realm] the thirty-seven groups, and the eighty-four thousand groups; all belonged to the Buddha's territory as newly cultivated fields of the Buddha's community. In any Buddhist restricted territory these days, however, there are no nuns or other females, no eight groups.

We may not hope for a more eminently pure community than that which existed at the time the Tathāgata dwelt in the world. Because this world is inhabited by celestial beings and demons [as well as human beings], the teaching and conversion within the Buddhist assemblies are done without distinction of one's own world or other worlds, or of the worlds of the thousand Buddhas of past, present, and future. If there were any difference in the teaching, you would know that the place where it was taught is not a Buddhist assembly.

The four fruits[65] are the ultimate stage. Whether it is the small vehicle or great vehicle, the merits of the ultimate stage are the same.

Now, there are many nuns who have acquired the four fruits. Whether it be here in the three realms, in Buddha lands in the ten directions, or in any other world, nuns have reached this stage. Who would hinder their practice [by forbidding them entrance to the restricted territories]? Also, the stage of wonderful enlightenment is the supreme stage.[66] At the time a female became a Buddha,[67] everything in the universe was completely understood. What person would hinder her, thinking that she had not truly come into this world? The merits [of her attainment] exist right now, illumining the whole universe, so even though you set up boundary lines, they are of no use.

Furthermore, would you hinder celestial females or demon females from entering? Neither celestial females nor demon females are of a species that can terminate their delusions, and they remain within the cycle of death and rebirth. Sometimes they violate the moral precepts, sometimes they do not. The same is true of human females and animal females; sometimes they violate the precepts, sometimes they do not. Who would get in the way of celestials or demons? They have already visited places where the Buddha taught the Dharma, and they have trained beside the Buddha. Who would believe the Buddhadharma was the real Dharma if there were a difference of place or a difference of teaching? To believe otherwise is nothing but the extreme stupidity of humans who are still deceived by their delusions and they are more trifling than someone who tries to pull the wool over someone's eyes.

In the ranks of Buddhists, in both the small vehicle and the great vehicle, there are monks, nuns, laymen, and laywomen. This has been known from ancient times among humans and celestial beings. The rank of nun surpasses that of even a great, world-conquering king or that of even Sakra, most powerful of the celestials. Consequently, there is nothing she has not accomplished. How much less can you compare the royalty and courtiers of some small, peripheral country with a nun! Yet we now see restricted territories that are forbidden to nuns but into which go rustics from the rice fields, woodcutters, and others, not to mention royalty, chief ministers of state, other officials, and counselors. If you compare nuns with rice farmers and the others, then what do superior and inferior mean from the standpoint of Buddhist practice and achieving certain ranks? Whether we are talking about worldly usage or Buddhist usage, farmers and others like them should not enter places that are forbidden to nuns. This extreme confusion still persists in this little country of ours. How pitiful that even though the venerable daughters of the compassionate Buddha have come to this small land, they find the doors of some places barred to them.

What is more, those who live in these so-called restricted territories do not themselves seem to dread the ten evils, and sometimes they commit the ten kinds of offense. Living as they do within a place of evil, they should not hate those who do not commit evil. Need I say that they should consider the five unpardonable crimes to be very grave? Those who live in the restricted territories should not commit such crimes. Demon territories such as these should be destroyed, and those who live in them ought to learn the Buddha's teaching. They should enter the Buddha's territory. This would be the way to repay the Buddha for his favors.

You predecessors of ours who held such opinions about women, I wonder if you understood the profound idea behind the establishment of Buddhist restricted territories. From whom did you inherit this territory? Who gave you *inka* [permission to teach]?

All those that are included in the great territories that were established by the Buddha—Buddhas, ordinary beings, the earth, the sky—are freed from the bonds that tie them to this world, and all return to the root of the wonderful Dharma of all the Buddhas. This being so, all those who once set foot in such a place receive the merits of the Buddha; that is, the merits of a nonrelapsing heart and the merits of purity [of body, mouth, and mind].

When one part of the universe is bound to the Dharma, everything in the universe is bound to the Dharma. When one kind is bound to the Dharma, all are bound to it. There are territories bound with water, bound with mind, and bound with space. This territory, it should be understood, has been transmitted through inheritance [from teacher to disciple] over the years. Even after one has sprinkled the body with pure, sweet water, paid reverence by taking the Triple Refuge, and so on up through cleansing the restricted territory, one should still recite the verse:

The territory of benevolence pervades the whole universe;
Being just as it is, it is bound to purity.

I wonder whether you predecessors of previous generations understood this deep meaning when you spoke of "restricted territory"? You probably would not understand that within a single restricted territory the whole universe is bound. You should understand that you have been imbibing the wine of the small vehicle and mistakenly think that your meager territory is a large one. I hope some day you will sober up from your intoxication with the wine of delusion and no longer transgress against the all-pervading territory—the great territory—of all the Buddhas. When you try to emancipate all sentient beings and gather them up, they will honor and venerate the merits acquired from teaching and conversion. Then no one will be able to say that you have not acquired the essence of the Way.

Shunjū

"SPRING AND FALL"

A CERTAIN MONK asked the great master Tung-shan, "When the cold or heat arrives, how can one avoid it?" The master answered, "Why don't you go to a place where there is no cold or heat?" "Where is this place where there is neither cold nor heat?" asked the monk. Said Tung-shan, "When it is cold, the cold kills the monk; when it is hot, the heat kills the monk."

Many people all the way up to the present have discussed the problem set forth in this dialogue. Nowadays, too, people should exert themselves diligently in solving this problem. The ancestors have invariably investigated this realm, and those who have investigated it are the ancestors. In both India and China, many of the Buddhas and ancestors of past and present have considered the comprehension of this problem to be the actualization of one's [original] face. Actualizing one's [original] face in terms of this problem has been the kōan of all the ancestors.

However, you too must fully clarify the real meaning of that monk's question, "When the cold or heat arrives, how can one avoid it?" It is nothing other than clarifying the problem of the time when cold surely comes or when heat surely comes. What is meant here by "cold" and "heat" is that they are the totality of cold and heat, both are just cold and heat as they really are. Because cold and heat are just that, when they come, they come from the head-crown of cold and heat as they really are. They are manifested from the eye-pupil of cold and heat just as they really are. This crown of the head is the sphere of cold and heat; within the pupil of the eye is the place of cold and heat.

Tung-shan's statement, "When it is cold, the cold kills the monk; when it is hot, the heat kills the monk," is a direct hint concerning the arrival of cold and heat. However, even though it is said that when the cold comes, the cold kills, this does not mean you should be trapped by words and think that the heat necessarily kills when it is hot. Therefore, when it is cold, be thoroughly cold, and when it is hot, be thoroughly hot. Though you may try to avoid either one, there is nothing but cold and heat. The cold is the twinkling eyes of the ancestors, and the heat is the warm flesh of Tung-shan.

The Zen master Ching-yin K'u-mu said this concerning the dialogue between Tung-shan and the monk: "Among many people who practice Zen it is sometimes said that since the monk's question landed him on the side of the conditioned, Tung-shan's answer got him back to the side of nonconditionality. The monk caught the drift of Tung-shan's words and fought his way back toward nonconditionality, and in the face of this development, Tung-shan in turn established himself once more on the side of the conditioned. Conjecturing in this way, they not only blaspheme the Buddha, they land in false views themselves. Haven't you ever heard the words of Chia-shan Shan-hui, who said, "The pleasure of hearing the explanations of ordinary people will grow to such an extent that it will make you ill"? When people who sincerely aspire to practice try to get to the bottom of Tung-shan's words, they must understand them by first experiencing enlightenment in his treasury of the true Dharma eye. Any other teaching of the ancestors is just the sound of a boiling pot. But still I ask you, in the end, "What kind of place is it where there is no cold or heat? Can you tell me?" A pair of birds make their nests in the jeweled tower; a pair of mandarin ducks are chained in the golden hall.

Zen master K'u-mu was in the lineage of Tung-shan, and he was outstanding among the old ancestral teachers. Many of those involved in training have tended to mistakenly interpret the teachings of Tung-shan from the standpoint of conditionality and nonconditionality, but Master K'u-mu clearly forbade it.[68] If the Buddha's teaching had been transmitted from the limited viewpoint of conditionality and nonconditionality, how would it ever have come down to the present time? However, stray cats and servant girls lacking in experience still do not get to the bottom of Tung-shan's words, and not having ever once experienced the essence of the Buddha, they are completely mistaken and try to guide people by explaining all of Tung-shan's teaching—everything from the conditioned and nonconditioned through the five ranks [describing the relative and absolute]. However, this is foolish talk, and you must not heed it. Just start at once to study the fact that it is Tung-shan's treasury of the true Dharma eye.

The Zen master Hung-chih of Mount T'ien-lung was a Dharma descendent of the priest Tan-hsia. His posthumous name was Cheng-chüeh. This is what he said about Tung-shan's teaching: "If we try to discuss it,[69] you and I are like a couple of checker players. When you oppose what I have played, I try to defeat you by maneuvering forward and backward. If you understand it in this way, you will understand Tung-shan's real meaning. However, I cannot help adding my own explanation. When you look at what is within, there is no more cold or heat than there is a drop of water in the ocean right in front of you. What I want to say is that since you can freely stoop over and pluck up the big turtle from the bottom of the ocean, I have to laugh to see you standing on the shore, trying to catch it with a fishing pole." Now, the example of playing checkers is quite appropriate, but what sort of thing is this business of two people playing? If you speak of two people playing, you are still caught in duality [literally, "there will be eight eyes"]. And if you are caught in duality, there is no checker game. How can there be? Therefore, shouldn't it rather be said that only one person is playing checkers and that he is his own opponent? However, with regard to Hung-chih's statement, "when you oppose me," you should ponder this with your hearts and bodies. The meaning of "when you oppose me" is that you are thoroughly you, and even now there is no one here called "me" here. Do not overlook the significance of "I try to defeat you." This is just muddiness of mind. The hiker washes his feet and he washes the tassels of his shoes. This is also like a jewel within a jewel. When it gleams, it illuminates others and it illuminates itself.

The Zen master Huan-wu of Mount Chia said, "The container makes the jewel run about and the jewel runs about within the container. There is the unconditioned within the conditioned and the conditioned within the unconditioned. It is like an antelope sleeping with his antlers hanging from tree branches so as not to leave any clues as to where he is, and the hunting dog searches in vain for him in the forest." The expression "the container makes the jewel run about" is a marvel of past and present times and is beyond comparison. In the past it was explained as meaning that the jewel that runs about in the vessel never stops looking. However, the antelope now hangs his antlers from the sky, and the forest is searching for the dog.

Zen Master Ming-chiao was the disciple of Chih-men Kuang-tsu. His posthumous name was Chung-hsien. He said, "This teaching kindly extended to the monk is as inaccessible as a ten-thousand-fathom cliff, and it is not restricted to conditioned and unconditioned. The old hill of lapis lazuli is illuminated by the moon, and the dog who howls at the moon vainly runs up the stairs of the old hall." Ming-chiao was in the third generation after Yun-men and it can be said that he cultivated the Way sufficiently. His expression, "This teaching kindly extended to the monk is as inaccessible as a ten-thousand-fathom cliff," may be said to reveal the incomparable realm, but this is not necessarily so.

Now, the circumstance of the monk's question and Tung-shan's answer neither speaks nor does not speak of "teaching"; the Buddha is not said to appear in the world nor said not to appear. How much less does this circumstance speak of conditioned and unconditioned! If you do not use such expressions as "conditioned" and "nonconditioned," you will cease to be unskillful with Tung-shan's kōan. You will never reach his realm if you do not use all your powers to penetrate the truth. Therefore, study this with all your strength, and stop saying that Tung-shan's teaching can be understood by means of the conditioned and nonconditioned, or of the five ranks, when there is no excuse for it.

The Zen master Ch'ang-ling said, "There is the nonconditioned within the conditioned and the conditioned within the nonconditioned, and they pervade the human world eternally. However often you may wish to return to the place where there is no cold or heat, you cannot return. The grass grows abundantly before the gate as it has since olden times." Now, although Ch'ang-ling is speaking to you about the conditioned and nonconditioned, he is just using them as the state of reality. It is not that they cannot be used in connection with reality, for if not, how could there be this "exists within the conditioned"?

The priest Ta-wei Fa-hsing said, "Tung-shan's answer pervades that place where there is no cold or heat, and he does this for your sake. The withered tree produces a single blossom. It is laughable to watch a person tearing apart the boat looking for the sword that fell into the water. Right now, he abides in the cold ashes."[70] These words freely go a little beyond Tung-shan's kōan.

The Zen master Chan-t'ang Wen-chun said, "When it is cold, everything is thoroughly cold; when it is hot, everything is thoroughly hot. Heat and cold originally have no connection. Running all over heaven and earth looking into mundane matters, the noble lord accepts a vulgar crown for his head." I would like to ask Chan-t'ang just what sort of thing is this "no connection"? Quickly, quickly, answer!

The Zen master Shou-chün said, "Tung-shan's teaching about the place where there is no cold or heat is a source of great delusion for monks without experience. If you move toward the fire when it is cold and cool yourself when it is hot, you will be able to avoid cold and heat for your whole life." Now, this Shou-chün was a teacher in the lineage of Wu-tsu Fa-yen, but his words are the words of a baby. However, the words "you will be able to avoid cold and heat for your whole life" contain in them the potential for revealing a deep meaning. "Whole life" means the totality of life. "Avoiding cold and heat" means dropping off mind and body.

In all these critical verses up to now, ancestral teachers of various times have tried to explain Tung-shan's statement, but they still fail to penetrate Tung-shan's realm. The reason for this is that in their everyday lives, these ancestral teachers did not really understand what cold and heat are, and so they spoke of either moving closer to a fire or cooling oneself. What a shame! I wonder if you, Shou-chün, studied the matter of what cold and heat are? How sad that the Way of the Buddha has become completely lost!

You should make a kōan of Tung-shan's statement, and make it your own problem, and so come to understand the meaning of cold and heat, experience the time of cold and heat, and use cold and heat as your own. If you still do not understand it, you should reflect upon yourself and consider your own past wickedness. Even people who are not Buddhists understand time, and there are holy people and wise people who can explain the myriad things—even wise people and fools are able to explain them. Do not explain the cold and heat that are a problem in Buddhism as being like the cold and heat as understood by foolish people. At any rate, just study the problem earnestly.

Shinjin Inga
"DEEP FAITH IN CAUSE AND EFFECT"

WHENEVER the Zen master Pai-chang preached the Dharma in the Dharma hall, there was always an old man there who respectfully listened to the Dharma teaching and then left with the monks. However, one day, when the monks left, he stayed behind. "Who is this standing before me?" asked the master. The old man answered, "I am not really a human being. Long, long ago, during the time of Kāshyapa Buddha, I lived here as chief priest of a monastery. One day a monk asked me, 'Does a person who has perfected his training and is enlightened remain subject to cause and effect or not?' I answered, 'He is not subject to cause and effect.' Because of this answer, I have spent five hundred lifetimes in the body of a fox. I now ask you respectfully to say some turning word [that will change my mental attitude][71] and free me from this fox body." Then he asked the master, "Is a person who has become enlightened subject to the law of cause and effect?" Pai-chang replied, "He does not ignore cause and effect." Upon hearing these words, the old man had a great satori. Bowing to Pai-chang, he said, "I am now liberated from the body of the fox, which you will find at the foot of the cliff near the monastery. May I be so bold as to request the chief priest to have it buried as you would a dead monk?"

The master had the *ino* [chief liturgist] strike the mallet and announce to the monks that there would be a funeral service for a dead monk right after the meal. The monks were quite agitated and wondered, "Since all the monks here in this monastery are healthy and there is no one in the infirmary, who could have died, that we must perform funeral services for a dead monk?" After they had eaten, the master took them to the foot of the cliff where, poking about with his staff, he found the remains of a fox. He had the body cremated in accordance with the custom among Buddhists.

That evening, during his talk in the Dharma hall, he spoke of the circumstances surrounding the cremation of the fox. Huang-po asked him, "The old man gave a wrong answer to the monk, and as a consequence, he had to abide in the body of a fox for five hundred lifetimes. But if he had not made a mistake, what would he have become?" Pai-chang said, "Come closer and I'll tell you." Huang-po came close to the master and suddenly slapped him on the cheek. Pai-chang clapped his hands and laughed. "I thought the foreigner's beard was red, but it was really a red-bearded foreigner." This story is recorded in the *Mumonkan* [The Gateless Gate].[72]

Monks in training do not understand the principle of cause and effect and consequently many have made the mistake of thoughtlessly doubting this principle. This is truly lamentable, for once bad habits begin to spread in the world, the Way of the ancestors begins to decline. To think that one is not subject to cause and effect is to deny cause and effect, and the result is that you fall into the realms of animals, the purgatories, and so on.

However, to affirm this great principle and say that one does not ignore cause and effect clearly indicates a deep faith in the principle of cause and effect. As a result, one can become liberated from suffering in this present lifetime. Do not have any doubt about the principle of cause and effect. Do not question it. Many who practice Zen these days do doubt it. How do I know they doubt it? They either believe that they are not subject to cause and effect, or else they believe the nature of this principle is such that no one can escape it anyway, so in either case, they deny cause and effect.

The nineteenth [Indian] ancestor, Kumārata, said, "There are three periods for the maturation of good and bad karma.[73] When we look at human life, we see that often the compassionate person suffers and dies, while the wicked person who gets along in the world by means of violence is happy and lives a long life. Also, the decent person is unhappy and wretched, while the wicked person who commits the five unpardonable offenses[74] without ever thinking twice about it is happy. This is the way it seems, and we may wonder why it is this way. When we study this situation, we see that the person who trains in a superficial way thinks that cause and effect have nothing to do with this life and that misery and happiness have nothing to do with cause and effect. This person does not understand that the law of cause and effect never deviates, any more than a shadow or echo deviates from its source. Nor does he understand that the law of cause and effect never lapses, even after millions of eons."

You should understand that none of the ancestors has ever denied the law of cause and effect. It is due to their own negligence that people who practice Zen these days do not understand the teachings of the compassionate ancestors. Negligent though they may be, they become self-styled teachers of men and gods, and thus they rob men and gods and are the sworn enemies of all real students. These fellows who crowd around younger students should not spread the false teaching that denies the principle of cause and effect. It is a wrong teaching because it is not the Dharma of the ancestors. If you become careless, you will fall utterly into this wrong view.

Certain monks in Sung China these days say, "We have acquired human form and have encountered the Dharma, but we still do not understand this present life or the future life. We understand that after that priest became a fox, he spent five hundred lifetimes in the body of a fox, but he did not become a fox as the result of karma. Even though he passed through the difficult barrier of practice and acquired supreme enlightenment, he did not remain in that state, but descended into the world of animals and was constantly reborn there."

This is the sort of thing taught by people who are called "great leaders of the world." But this explanation is not in accordance with the essence of the ancestors. There are those who have the supernatural power to know their past lives, whether as humans, animals, or some other form of sentient life. However, this supernatural power is not acquired by becoming enlightened in the Dharma; rather, it is the result of bad karma in past lives. Shakyamuni himself taught this principle extensively. That people do not understand it is due to their neglect of practice. Truly it is a shame, for even though one knows a thousand past lives or even ten thousand past lives, this is not really knowing the Dharma. Even non-Buddhists sometimes know the events of eighty thousand eons. However, this is still not the Dharma. Even if you can understand a little of the events of five hundred lifetimes, it is not really much of an ability.

Zen monks in China nowadays display a dismal ignorance of the fact that this teaching of not being subject to cause and effect is an incorrect teaching. What a pity! They are worthy of the Buddha's teaching, correctly transmitted from ancestor to ancestor, yet they become people who negate the law of cause and effect. Those who practice Zen should stir themselves and clarify this principle of cause and effect right now. Pai-chang's assertion that one does not ignore cause and effect clarifies this principle. Therefore, the principle according to which one acquires a certain result on the basis of a cause in the form of action is quite clear, and it is the truth of the Buddha and ancestors. Generally speaking, if you have still not sufficiently clarified the Buddhadharma, you ought not to preach the Dharma rashly and heedlessly to others.

Nāgārjuna, our ancestral teacher,[75] said, "The non-Buddhists say that if you deny the law of cause and effect in this life, then the present life and the future life are destroyed. If you deny that the appearance of all the Buddhas in the world due to their enlightenment results from cause and effect, then you negate the Three Jewels, the four holy truths, and the four fruits of the monk." You must clearly understand that if you deny cause and effect in the world or in the supramundane realm, you have become a non-Buddhist. Saying, "The present world does not exist," you believe that while the body appears here in this world, the self abides in a permanent, immutable world. The self is identified with the mind. The mind is explained as something remaining apart from the body. This is the way in which non-Buddhists think about the body.

Or else it is sometimes said that when a person dies, his self returns to the great ocean of essence. Therefore, if one naturally returns to the ocean of essence even though he has not cultivated the Dharma, he no longer transmigrates in the world of birth and death, and therefore there is no afterworld. This is the annihilationist view of non-Buddhists. Even if in appearance he looks like a Buddhist monk, the fool who believes such a teaching is not at all a son of the Buddha. He is truly a non-Buddhist. The idea that the present world and the afterworld do not exist because there is no law of cause and effect is incorrect. The denial of cause and effect results from not studying with a real teacher. If you study for a long time with a real teacher, you will not fall into wrong views that deny cause and effect. You should deeply believe in the compassionate teaching of Nāgārjuna and humbly accept it.

The great master Hsüan-chüeh was a prominent disciple of Zen Master Ts'ao-ch'i. Earlier, he had studied the *Lotus Sutra* of the T'ien-t'ai sect, and he was a fellow student of the great master Tso-chi Hsüan-lang. As Hsüan-chüeh read the *Nirvāna Sūtra,* a golden light filled his room. When this happened, Hsüan-chüeh was enlightened in the principle of the Birthless. Thereupon, he continued his efforts, and visited the Zen master Hui-neng on Mount Ts'ao-ch'i to demonstrate his enlightenment to the Sixth Ancestor. Hui-neng approved his satori and transmitted the Dharma to him. Afterward, Hsüan-chüeh composed the *Cheng tao ko.* In it are these lines:

A liberal emptiness negates cause and effect;
Like flourishing grasses and rippling waves, calamities come.

You should understand that if you deny cause and effect, you will invite calamity. All the old Buddha ancestors clarified the matter of cause and effect. However, Zen monks nowadays who come after them are deluded about cause and effect. In this state of affairs, people who arouse a pure thought of enlightenment and attempt to study the Dharma for the sake of the Dharma should clarify the principle of cause and effect in the same way the old ancestors did. "No cause, no effect" is something said by non-Buddhists.

The Zen master Hung-chih Cheng-chüeh explained Pai-chang's statement about cause and effect with these verses from his *Ts'ung yung lu:*

A foot of water becomes a foot of waves;
So nothing could be done about the five hundred lives as a fox.

Arguing "is not subject to causation" or "does not ignore it,"
As of old, they still fall into a den of complexities and cannot
    escape.
Ha-ha-ha! I wonder if you understand?
O monks, if you have eliminated false thoughts and are free,
You will have no difficulty with my [mindless] "goo-goo, nah-nah"!
Sing before the spirits and dance with the earth deities
And you will be able to compose your own tune.
Then you and I, united, will clap hands joyously,
Singing "tum-tiddly-um tum-tiddly-um sum."

Now Hung-chih's phrase "Arguing 'is not subject to causation' or 'does not ignore it,' they still fall into a den of complexities," means nothing less than that not being subject to cause and effect and not ignoring cause and effect are to be considered the same.

At any rate, this principle of cause and effect is still not thoroughly clear. The reason is that even though it is a fact that the old man was freed from the body of the fox, the story did not say that after being freed he was reborn in the human world, or that he was reborn in the celestial realm, or in the realm of animals, and so on. If after leaving the body of the fox he had been reborn in one of the fortunate destinations, he would have become a human or a celestial being. If he had been reborn in an evil destination, he would have been reborn in the purgatories, among hungry spirits, as an animal, or as a fighting *asura*. When he was freed from the body of the fox, he had to be reborn someplace. If you say that upon dying a living being returns to the great ocean of essential being, nirvana, or that he returns to the Great Self, that is the incorrect view of non-Buddhists.

The Zen master Chia-shan Yüan-wu explained the situation in the following verses:

When a fish swims, the water becomes muddied;
When a bird flies, its feathers fall.
Just as an object is reflected in a polished mirror,
Nothing can escape the law of cause and effect.
Just as not a single thing can be hidden in the vast sky,

The five hundred lives as a fox came from the great activity
    of cause and effect.
Swift lightning may rend the mountains, the winds may make
    the seas tremble.
But just as gold refined a hundred times still retains its color,
The activity of cause and effect is eternal and unchanging.

In these verses, there is some remnant of the tendency to deny cause
and effect, and there is also some remainder of the eternalist view.
The Zen master Ching-shan Ta-hui says,

The turning phrases "is not subject" and "does not ignore"
    are identical
In the same way a stone head and the earth spirit are the same.
The freedom from the fox body after five hundred lives
Was like the pulverizing of a silver mountain.
Someone hears such a doctrine and claps his hands joyously
And with shaking belly laughs uproariously—it is Pu-tai.[76]

People in China in the present time consider these men to be
splendid teachers. However, Ta-hui's opinion is still far from the
teaching of skillful means, for it falls into the view of naturalness
held by non-Buddhists and does not exemplify a deep faith in cause
and effect.

All in all, more than thirty priests have composed verses or kōans
in connection with Pai-chang's fox, but every one of them thought
that the words "is not subject to cause and effect" deny the law of
cause and effect. What a pity! These men did not clarify the principle of cause and effect, and while they argue "does" or "does not,"
they fruitlessly waste their lives in the very midst of life. In studying
the Dharma, the first thing to do is to clarify the principle of cause
and effect. The kind of people who deny it produce extremely bad
wrong views and cut off the roots of goodness and end up as people
who are hard to help.

The principle of cause and effect is clear, and it is evident everywhere. The person who does evil falls into the purgatories, and the
person who cultivates good is freed from all suffering, and this truth

*Ta-Hui is
one of the
great Chin masters*

deep faith

123

never varies by so much as an inch. If this principle were destroyed, the Buddhas would not appear in the world, and Bodhidharma would not have gone to China. Therefore, living beings would not see the Buddha or hear the Dharma. The principle of cause and effect cannot be explained by such people as Confucius and Lao-tzu; only the Buddhas and ancestors have explained it and correctly transmitted it. Zen students during the time of the decline of the Dharma[77] are unhappy and cannot find a real teacher; consequently, they cannot hear the real Dharma. Thus, they cannot come to clearly understand the principle of cause and effect. Moreover, if they deny this principle, then as a result of their offense, they cannot avoid the calamities, numerous as blades of grass in the fields, that befall them. Even though one commits no other bad karma besides denying cause and effect, the pain that comes from just this one wrong view is great.

Therefore, those who study Zen in the Buddhadharma may wish to start by arousing the thought of enlightenment and repaying the kindness of the Buddha and ancestors, but first of all they should clearly understand the principle of cause and effect.

Nyorai Zenshin
"THE TATHĀGATA'S WHOLE BODY"

O N ONE OCCASION when the Buddha was staying at the Vulture Peak in Rājagriha, he spoke to the bodhisattva, the mahasattva, Bhaisajya-rāja: "O Bhaisajya-rāja, in every lifetime you should discuss, read, recite, and copy this sutra, and wherever this sutra is found, you should build a stupa higher and broader than all the others, adorned with the seven precious stones. But you should not place the relics of the Buddha within it. Why? Because the whole body of the Tathāgata is already within it. Therefore, this stupa should be honored, revered, and praised with offerings of flowers, incense, jewels, canopies, banners, music, and songs. When people see this stupa, and pay homage to it and honor it, all these people, you should know, will be close to supreme enlightenment."[78] What is spoken of here as the "sutra" is discussion, reading, chanting, and copying. The mark of ultimate reality that all things have[79] is also the sutra. As for the "stupa that one should build of the seven precious stones," it is also the mark of ultimate reality of all things. The size of this extremely tall and broad stupa is the size of the mark of ultimate reality that all things have [that is to say, it is markless]. "The whole body of the Tathāgata is already within the stupa" means that the sutra itself is the whole body.

Therefore, the acts of discussing the sutra, reading it, chanting it, copying it, and so on, are themselves the whole body of the Tathāgata. You should honor, revere, and praise it with flowers, incense, jewels, canopies, banners, music, and songs. It is said that one should honor, revere, and praise it with heavenly flowers, heavenly incense, heavenly canopies, and so on. All these are the mark of ultimate reality that all things have. But they can also be the very best flowers, the best incense, the best robes, the best clothing, and so on, of the human world. All these are also the mark of ultimate reality. The acts of honoring and revering are all the mark of ultimate reality. You should understand that when it is said that a stupa should be built but that the Tathāgata's relics should not be placed in it, what is meant is that the sutra itself is the relics of the Tathāgata; it is the Tathāgata's whole body. There are no greater merits than those of directly hearing the golden words of the Buddha when he preaches the Dharma. [The Sutra itself is the direct sound of the golden words; they are the Buddha's whole body.] You should accumulate merits as fast as you can and be diligent in heaping them up [by reading, chanting, and copying the sutras, which are worthy of honor, reverence, and praise]. If there are people who honor and revere this stupa, you should understand that this is "all are close to *anuttara samyak sambodhi.*"[80] When beings see this stupa, they should sincerely pay homage to it and revere it. They will be close to anuttara samyak sambodhi. This "close" has nothing to do with intervals such as close or far; it is the anuttara samyak sambodhi that we may say "all are close to." When we now see this sutra received and upheld, read and recited, understood, preached, and copied, "we can see the stupa." It is delightful that "all are close to anuttara samyak sambodhi."

This being so, the sutra is the whole body of the Tathāgata. Paying homage to the sutra is paying homage to the Tathāgata. Coming into contact with the sutra is meeting the Tathāgata. The sutra is the Buddha's relics. This being so, the relics are this sutra. Even though you may understand that this sutra is the relics of the Buddha, if you do not know that the relics are the sutra, it cannot be said that you know the Buddha Way yet. The mark of reality of all things in the present time is the sutra. The human world, the heavens, the realms of the sea and space, other realms, all are the mark of ultimate reality. They are the sutra; they are the bone relics.

You should receive and support, read and recite, explain, preach, and copy the bone relics, and in so doing become enlightened. This is being in accord with the sutra. There are relics of ancient Buddhas, relics of Buddhas of the present time, relics of *shravakas* [hearers of the Dharma] and pratyekabuddhas [solitary realizers], relics of world rulers, and relics of the kings of lions. There are also the relics of wooden Buddhas, relics of Buddhas painted on silk, and there are human relics. Nowadays in Sung China, the relics of Buddhas and ancestors who lived at various times appear. There have been many relics that have appeared after the Buddhas and ancestors have died. All are the sutra.

Shakyamuni Buddha once spoke to a great crowd, saying "The life-duration that I acquired from the merits of practicing the path of the bodhisattva is eternal and not yet terminated."[81] The eight *koki* and four *shō*[82] of relics that now remain are the Buddha's life. The lifespan resulting from the merits of the original bodhisattva practices is not limited in size by even such things as the size of the universe. It transcends this limit; it is limitless. This is the whole body of the Tathāgata, it is this sutra.

The bodhisattva Jnanakara said, "I see that even though for countless eons Shakyamuni Buddha has practiced difficult and painful practices, accumulated merits, and sought the Way of the bodhisattva, and that even though he is now a Buddha he still practices diligently. I see that in all worlds, from those the size of the whole universe down to those the size of a mustard seed, there is no place the bodhisattva does not abandon his own body and life in order to help living beings. All this is done for the sake of living beings, and afterward he will achieve perfect enlightenment."[83]

You should clearly understand that this universe is a fragment of the red heart, and space is contained within the hollow of the hand. They are the whole body of the Tathāgata. This has nothing to do with the Buddha's renouncing his body or not renouncing his body. The relics of the Buddha are neither prior to his appearance in the world nor do they come after his disappearance, for it is not really a question of whether they are or are not the Buddha. The long eons of difficult and painful practices are the activity of the womb of the Buddha, they are the activity of the innermost being of the Buddha; that is to say, they are the Buddha's skin, flesh, bone, and marrow. When it is said that these practices have not ceased even for a second, it means that even though he is perfectly enlightened, he still practices vigorously, and he continues forever even though he converts the whole universe. This activity is the whole body of the Tathāgata.

Gyōji
"CONTINUOUS PRACTICE"

IN THE GREAT Way of the Buddha ancestors there is always supreme continuous practice that is the Way without beginning or end. Arousing the thought of enlightenment, practice, enlightenment, and nirvana have not the slightest break, but are a continuous practice that goes on forever. Therefore, this continuous practice is neither one's own effort nor someone else's effort; it is pure, continuous practice that transcends the opposition of self and others.

The merit of this continuous practice upholds oneself and others, because due to one's own effort, all worlds in the universe all the way up to the heavenly abodes immediately share in its benefits. Even though you may not be aware of it yourself and others may not be aware of it, that is the way it is. Therefore, because of the continuous practice of all the Buddhas and ancestors, our own continuous practice becomes a reality and the Way of the Buddhas is opened for us. Because of our own continuous practice, the continuous practice of all the Buddhas and ancestors is manifested, and the Way of all the Buddhas is opened. Because of our own continuous practice, there are the merits of the Way that is without beginning. Because of this continuous practice, each former Buddha and ancestor abides as a Buddha, transcends Buddhahood, is resolved as a Buddha, and is perfected as a Buddha endlessly.

Because of this continuous practice, there are the sun, moon, and stars. Because of this continuous practice, there are the earth and sky, and the heart within and the body without, the four elements and the five skandhas. Continuous practice is not something ordinary people are fond of, but nevertheless, it is the true refuge for everyone. Because of this continuous practice of the Buddhas of past, present, and future, the Buddhas of past, present, and future are manifested. The merits of this continuous practice are sometimes apparent, and so beings arouse the thought of enlightenment and begin to practice. Sometimes these merits of continuous practice are not evident, and so beings do not see and hear them and do not come to understand them. But you should understand that even though these merits are not revealed, they are not concealed.

When the continuous practice that manifests itself is truly continuous practice, you may be unaware of what circumstances are behind it, and the reason why you do not notice them is that to understand such a thing is not that special. Conditional arising is continuous practice, but continuous practice is not conditionally generated, and this you should diligently seek to understand. It is this way because continuous practice is not dominated by any other thing. This kind of continuous practice that reveals continuous practice is nothing more than our continuous practice *now*. The immediate *now* of continuous practice is not something that existed in me from before. The time called "now" is not born from continuous practice. The time when continuous practice is manifested is what we call "now." Consequently, one day of continuous practice by us becomes the seed of all the Buddhas; one day of continuous practice by us is the continuous practice of all the Buddhas. On the basis of this continuous practice, all the Buddhas are manifested. Not to continuously practice what is to be continuously practiced is to hate the Buddha, not venerate the Buddha; not to continuously practice what is to be continuously practiced is to hate continuous practice, not be born with the Buddha and die with the Buddha. Not to continuously practice what is to be continuously practiced is to not learn with the Buddha and not practice with the Buddha. Opening up enlightenment in this present time and letting go of enlightenment is the action of continuous practice. Becoming a Buddha and transcending Buddhahood is the action of continuous practice.

For this reason, you may sometimes try to conceal the deluded thought of avoiding continuous practice when you neglect it by saying that "even avoiding continuous practice is itself continuous practice." But this is a half-hearted continuous practice, and it cannot be considered seeking continuous practice. Truly, it is like a poor person throwing away his inheritance and wandering off to some other land. Even though when you are distressed the wind and rain do not rob you of life and body, still the familial inheritance will be lost. Therefore, continuous practice should never be neglected for even a second.

Our compassionate father and great teacher, Shakyamuni Buddha, went into the mountains when he was nineteen and began continuous practice, and at the age of thirty, he engaged in continuous practice that perfected his practice along with that of the earth and all sentient beings. Up to the age of eighty, he practiced continuously in the mountains and in monasteries. He never returned to the palace of his father or resumed his position as a prince. For his whole life he never wore new monk's robes or had a new alms bowl. Not for a day, not for a moment, was he ever alone, but constantly he taught others and received them in the Dharma. He did not ever reject the veneration of humans or divine beings, nor was he ever upset at abuse from the followers of other teachings. The teachings and conversion activities of his whole lifetime were nothing but continuous practice. Keeping his robes clean and begging for his food were nothing but continuous practice.

The eighth ancestor [after the seven ancient Buddhas and Shakyamuni], Mahākāshyapa, was Shakyamuni's heir. In a previous life he had engaged in the practice of the twelve austerities as his continuous practice, and he was never negligent. He engaged in the twelve austerities as follows:

1. He did not accept invitations to eat at the homes of laymen, but every day he begged his food, and he did not eat the remains of the monks' one daily meal.

2. He lived in the mountains and never stayed in people's houses, counties, prefectures, or villages.

3. He did not beg for robes when he met people, nor did he take them if they were offered. He took the clothes off dead bodies, mended them, and wore them.

4. He stayed in fields and beneath trees.

5. He ate one meal a day.

6. He did not sleep on a broad bed. He continued to sit, and if he grew sleepy he walked around.

7. He owned only three robes and did not use bedding.

8. He lived on the sides of hills, not in temples, and he did not live among people. He did zazen while gazing at the bones of the dead, always seeking the truth.

9. He wished only to be by himself and did not want to be with people. Also, he did not sleep among others.

10. When he had eaten some fruits and nuts, he would eat some rice, and then he would eat no more.

11. He desired to live only in wild places, and he never stayed in huts under the trees.

12. He ate neither meat nor dairy products, nor did he ever rub hemp oil on his body.

These are the twelve austerities. He observed them faithfully for a whole lifetime, never backsliding. Even after he inherited the treasury of the true Dharma eye from the Buddha, he never gave up the observance of these austerities. Once the Buddha remarked to him, "You are already quite old, please eat the regular monks' food as well as nuts and fruit." Mahākāshyapa replied, "If you had not appeared in the world, I would have been a pratyekabuddha[84] dwelling alone in mountains and forests. Now, because you have appeared in the world, I have acquired the nourishment of the truth. In order to observe continuous practice, I will not eat monk's food." The Buddha praised him for this.

Mahākāshyapa once grew quite emaciated because of his austerities, and when some monks saw him, they mocked him. The Buddha courteously sat Mahākāshyapa beside him on his own seat. So Mahākāshyapa sat on the same seat with the Buddha. He was the elder member of the Buddha's order, and all the circumstances of his whole lifetime of continuous practice cannot be completely told.

For his whole life, the tenth ancestor, Pārshva, did not rest his ribs on the ground in order to lie down. Such practices, even though they continued until he was eighty, culminated in enlightenment and in his becoming an ancestral teacher. Because he did not foolishly waste time, in three short years of intense effort he came to correctly transmit the Dharma treasury of the true teaching of enlightenment. This honored one was in his mother's womb for sixty years, and when he was born he already had white hair. He was called the Rib Saint because he vowed never to lie down, but rested only on an armrest. In the dark his hands emitted flashes of light, which he used to help him read the scriptures and treatises. He exhibited these supernatural powers, which he possessed naturally. Now when the Rib Saint was eighty, he renounced the world and made his home departure. However, some young people in the city criticized this, saying, "You are just a senile old man. How did you get to be so stupid? Those who make their home departure do two things: they practice zazen and chant the scriptures. Now that you are so old, you must not behave in this manner any more. You left home and joined the Buddha's order only in order to get something to eat." The Rib Saint heard their criticism, thanked them, and made this vow: "If I do not master the three parts of the canon,[85] cut off all the desires of the three realms,[86] obtain the six supernatural powers, and make the eight liberations my own,[87] I will never use an armrest." From then on, he was careful about wasting time, and even if he was walking about, he meditated, so that every day he was engaged in meditation whether he was sitting, doing things, going out, or returning. In the daytime, he did walking meditation, sitting meditation, and studied the scriptures, and at night, he did sitting meditation; day and night for three years he maintained his continuous practice without a break. Consequently, he mastered the three parts of the canon, cut off the desires of the three worlds, and acquired the power of the three lores of the arhat.[88] When others heard of this, they praised him and called him the Rib Saint.

The Rib Saint was born after being in the womb for sixty years: I wonder if he didn't practice intensely while still in the womb? After he was born, when he reached eighty, he aroused the thought of enlightenment and made his home departure for the first time. This was one hundred and forty years from the time he was conceived. Truly, he was a rare, outstanding man of talent. He was older than any of his Dharma contemporaries, for he had grown old in the womb, and he continued to grow old after he was born. However, he took people's criticism to heart when he left the home life, and because he achieved the intention of his vow of home departure and acquiring the Way, after three years his practice was completed. No one who tries to do this sort of thing will speak unkindly of his example. Do not think ill of those who are very old.

It is difficult to investigate this life of ours or to thoroughly comprehend it. Is it life, or is it not life? Is it old age or is it not old age? In accordance with different viewpoints, these things are not at all identical, and the viewpoints themselves differ according to the individual's environment and abilities. If you want to understand such things, be determined and diligent in your practice. You should understand that life and death in their true form exist only within your practice, and that your diligent practice does not exist within life and death. Nowadays, when people reach the age of fifty or sixty or seventy or eighty, they stop practicing; this is at the very limit of stupidity. No matter how many years you have lived up to now, those years are nothing but thoughts in your mind, and you do not understand them in terms of practice. Do not look back on these years or pay any attention to them, but just make a diligent effort in your practice. Be like the Rib Saint. Do not have any regrets about this present fleeting life, which is no more than a handful of earth from a cemetery, and do not look backward at it. If you do not carry out your resolution, who is going to pity whom? You should try to see just how quickly this ownerless corpse is aimlessly scattered on the wild fields.

The sixth [Chinese] ancestor, Hui-neng, was a woodcutter in Hsin-chou, and was quite unlearned. He lost his father when he was young, and he was reared and cared for by his aged mother. In order to care for his mother, he made a living from the same wood-cutting his father had done. One day, at a crossroads, he heard a passage being recited from the Diamond Sutra, and he left his mother at once and began to seek the Dharma. He was a man who was rarely seen, and a preeminent follower of the Way. Perhaps it was easy for Hui-k'o [the second Chinese ancestor] to cut off his arm in search of the Dharma, but Hui-neng's cutting off of the bonds of love must have been extremely difficult, for I think that abandoning love for one's parents in this way is not easy. For eight months after he joined Hung-jen's group on Mount Huang-mei, he neither slept nor rested but pounded rice all night. As a result, he was correctly transmitted Hung-jen's Dharma in the night. Even after receiving the Dharma, he walked with the same mortar on his back and pounded rice for eight years. He became the chief priest of a monastery and a preacher of the Dharma for people, yet he did not get rid of the mortar. This is indeed rare continuous practice in this world.

Ma-tsu of Chiang-hsi did zazen for twenty years. Thus, he received *inka* from Nan-yüeh. Even when he succeeded Nan-yüeh and taught the Dharma to others, he was still never negligent about doing zazen. He set an example for those who were learning Zen for the first time, and when it was time for work, he started to work first. Even when he grew old, he did not neglect this. Those of the famous present-day Rinzai tradition are descended from Ma-tsu.

Yün-yen and Tao-wu practiced together on Mount Yo, made a vow together and for forty years, until they died, hardly ever laid down to sleep, but continued to practice the Way single-mindedly. In this way, they transmitted the great Dharma to the great master Tung-shan Wu-pen. Tung-shan said, "I wanted to practice the Way and do zazen a little, and already I have twenty years worth." This has been passed down to the present time.

When the great master Hung-chüeh of Yün-chü Mountain was staying in the Three Peaks Hermitage, a celestial being would send him food out of respect. The master visited Tung-shan, was enlightened in the great Dharma, and again returned to his hermitage. Again, the celestial being brought food, and though he called on the master, for three days he could not see him. The master no longer needed the help of this celestial being and tried only to attain the Buddhadharma. You should think about the constancy of his determination to practice.

After Zen master Pai-chang had been Ma-tsu's attendant, there was not a day up to the day he died when he did not exert himself on behalf of those studying under him. As for the precedent he left us in his saying, "A day without work, a day without eating," Pai-chang was already an old man when he said this and had undergone many years of strenuous practice. Still, he worked hard in the fields with the younger men in training. The monks lamented over this and felt sorry for him, and they tried to make him stop working, but he would not stop. One day when Pai-chang was working, a monk hid the tools he was using and would not show them to the old master. So for that whole day, the master did not eat, because he was disappointed in not being able to join the monks in the fields. This is the story behind his "A day without work, a day without eating." In present day Sung China, in the tradition of Lin-Chin and in all monasteries everywhere, many constantly put into practice this deep teaching of Pai-chang.

While Ching-ch'ing was serving as chief priest at a certain monastery, a guardian spirit of the earth was never able to see his form. The reason was that he couldn't detect the whereabouts of the chief priest while he was working.

Zen master I-chung of Mount Shan-p'ing also had previously received food from a celestial being. However, after the master saw Ta-tien, the celestial being could not see him when he looked for him. The chief priest, the later Ta-wei, remarked, "I have eaten the food of Mount Wei for twenty years, but because every bit of it went back into the latrines of Mount Wei, I did not take a thing. I did not even follow the teachings of Mount Wei. I am not such a simpleton as to take the guidance of others. I just worked as a cowherd for twenty years, taking care of an ox." You should understand that he was able to take care of this ox through his twenty years of continuous practice on Mount Wei. This master had formerly studied under Pai-chang. Just quietly picture to yourselves the circumstances of these twenty years of practice and do not forget them. Even though there are some who cultivate the Way of Mount Wei, not receiving the teachings of Mount Wei at all and continuously practicing the Buddha Way through work is truly rare.

The great master Chen-chi Ts'ung-shen [called Chao-chou], of Kuan-yin temple in Chao-chou, was sixty-one years old when he first aroused the thought of enlightenment and resolved to seek the

Way. He went on a pilgrimage carrying a priest's staff and a bowl for cleaning himself, and walking everywhere, said to himself, "If I meet someone who is superior to me, even if she is a seven-year-old girl, I will ask her for the Way, and even if he is a hundred-year-old man, if he is my inferior, I will teach him." He studied Nan-chüan's Dharma and practiced for twenty years. When he was eighty, he became chief priest of the Kuan-yin Temple, where he was the guide for the world for forty years. During that time, he didn't send a single letter to any of the families who supported the monastery in order to get donations. The meditation hall was not large, nor were there even any stands in front of and behind the hall where the monks could wash their faces and so on. One time, a leg of his seat broke off. So Chao-chou bound a piece of partially burned wood to the seat and kept it like this for a long time. The monk in charge of these matters wanted to replace the leg of the seat, but Chao-chou refused. You should make the traditions of these excellent Buddhas and ancestors models for your own lives.

It was after he was eighty that Chao-chou became chief priest at Kuan-yin Monastery in Chao-chou, and after his master instructed him in the Way, he correctly transmitted the Buddha Way. Everyone called him the "Old Buddha." Those who did not correctly transmit the Buddha Way [to themselves] must have been weaker than this master as far as the Dharma is concerned. Those who were not yet eighty years old must have been stronger and healthier than the master. Now, when we compare ourselves, who are strong and healthy, to this old teacher, we certainly do not come up to his standards with respect to the Buddha Way. Therefore, we must be diligent in our practices and practice continuously.

For forty years Chao-chou did not store up worldly goods, and every day he lacked sufficient rice. So, he either gathered chestnuts and ate them, or else he ate food given to him by the monks. Truly, all these are excellent examples of the lives of our predecessors, and excellent examples of practice by the Buddha's disciples. Once, Chao-chou said to the monks, "If you do not leave the monastery for your whole life and do not say a word for five or ten years, no one will be able to call you wicked. On the contrary, even all the Buddhas will not be able to call you anything."

These are golden words that illustrate continuous practice. You should understand that even though you may seem to be stupid because you are silent for five or ten years, people will not call you wicked in your silence. This is the meritorious act of not leaving the monastery. This not leaving the monastery for your whole life is itself the very form of continuous practice. The Buddha Way is like this. However, when you do not hear the sound of the Buddha's teaching, this is not to be considered the same as the non-evil of silence. But the supreme wonder of continuous practice is nothing other than not leaving the monastery, and not leaving the monastery is the total expression of dropping off mind and body. Stupid people do not understand this non-evil, nor do they make it known to others, because they cannot hear the Dharma preached within silence. The reason they do not teach this non-evil of silence is because they are themselves deluded. Those who do not understand that this is non-evil and do not teach it are to be pitied. The continuous practice of not leaving the monastery should be continuously and quietly practiced. Do not fly about willy-nilly as if blown by the east wind or west wind. If you possess the merit of continuous practice—of not leaving the monastery for five or ten years—to the extent that you do not even notice the spring breezes or autumn moon, you will be emancipated from the spring breezes and autumn moon. The realm of this continuous practice is unknown by us, and we do not understand it. This present moment of continuous practice should be engraved on your hearts as something to be greatly prized. Do not think that this silence is useless and empty. Entering the monastery and doing zazen in silence, or leaving the monastery and going all about, are both the form of the continuous practice of the monastery. This continuous practice of not leaving the monastery is the realm of freedom from conditions, in the same way that the sky is free from the tracks of flying birds; it is the realm where one is completely one with the whole universe. The whole universe is the monastery.

Ta-mei Mountain is in the prefecture of Ch'in-yüan. The person who founded the Hu-sheng Monastery was the Zen master Fa-ch'ang. He was from Hsiang-yang. Once he paid a visit to Ma-tsu and asked him, "What is the Buddha?" Ma-tsu replied, "The mind just as it is is the Buddha." Thereupon, Fa-ch'ang was enlightened. Then he went to the top of Ta-mei Mountain, where he stayed in a grass hermitage far away from people. He ate the seeds of cedar trees and wore the leaves of lotuses that grew abundantly in a pond on the mountain. There he did zazen and struggled for more than thirty years. Though he was lacking in worldly things, he never concerned himself with this and he completely forgot time. He was aware of nothing but the alternating greening and yellowing of the mountains all around him. When you think about it, this life of great poverty was pitiful.

When the master did zazen, he placed an eight-inch-high iron pagoda on top of his head, as if he were wearing a crown. He did this so that he would have to stay awake in order to prevent the pagoda from falling to the ground. This pagoda is still at the monastery of Hu-sheng, and it is taken out from time to time to serve as a reminder. Up to the time of his death, the master never forgot this practice.

When many years had passed, a monk who was studying with Zen master Yen-kuan came to the mountain and poked about with his traveling staff, becoming confused about where the path was. Without being aware of it, he stumbled upon the master's hermitage. Consequently, without intending it, he met the master. He asked Fa-ch'ang, "Chief Priest, how much time has passed since you began living here in these mountains?" The master replied, "All I know is the green and yellow of these mountains." Again the monk asked, "Which direction is the path out of these mountains?" The master answered, "Just follow the stream." The monk thought that this was a wonderful answer, and when he returned to Yen-kuan and told him about it, Yen-kuan said, "Long ago, when I was in Chiang-hsi, I happened to meet a monk like that, but afterward, I heard no more about him. I wonder if this is the same monk?" Thereupon he sent a monk to ask the master to come down from the mountain, but Fa-ch'ang refused to come. So, Yen-kuan composed a poem and sent it to him. The poem read,

The stump of the dead tree stands in the cold forest;
Even if it is exposed to the spring warmth, its heart is not moved.

Since no one takes notice of it, it being so stiff and hard,
Perhaps the carpenter will not want to use it.

Once more, Fa-ch'ang did not accept the invitation. Then he decided to move deeper into the mountains, and he composed a poem that said:

One cannot cut all the lotuses in the pond;
One cannot eat all the pine seeds.
Since the world has discovered my dwelling so easily,
I shall move my hermitage deeper into the mountains.

Later, Ma-tsu had a need to know the extent of Fa-ch'ang's attainment, so he sent a monk to find out. The monk asked Fa-ch'ang, "O Chief Priest, since you studied under Ma-tsu earlier, what principle did you acquire, and why did you come to live in these mountains?" The master replied, "My teacher, Ma-tsu, told me that the mind just as it is is the Buddha, and that is the reason I live here in these mountains." The monk said, "But recently the Buddhadharma has changed." "How is it different?" asked Fa-ch'ang. Said the monk, "Nowadays, Ma-tsu says that it is neither mind nor Buddha." To this, the master exclaimed, "That old fellow is still pulling the wool over everybody's eyes, eh? He can do whatever he wishes with this business of 'neither mind nor Buddha,' but all I care about right now is, 'The mind is the Buddha.'" The monk returned to Ma-tsu and told him about all this, and Matsu said, "The fruit of the plum is ripe."[89]

The whole world knows about these events. T'ien-lung was the excellent disciple of Zen Master Fa-ch'ang. Chü-tzu was another Zen man who dipped deeply into Fa-ch'ang's stream. Kya-chi, the Korean monk, transmitted the master's teaching and became the first ancestor of Zen in Korea. Consequently, everyone in the Zen tradition in Korea these days is drinking from the long stream of this master.

Even prior to his birth, a tiger and an elephant became the master's attendants, and they never quarreled together. When the master died, the tiger and elephant carried rocks and mud and made a tomb for the master. This grave still exists at Hu-sheng Monastery. This master's continuous practice is praised unanimously by people who call him a preeminent master of past and present. Those who are slight in intelligence do not understand that this is to be praised. To think that it is all right to covet fame and fortune in the Dharma is the ignorant idea of shallow people.

The Zen master Fa-yen, of the Monastery of the Five Ancestors, said, "When my own master, Pai-yün Shou-tuan, first went to live on Yang-ch'i Mountain, the rafters of the old building were badly damaged, and the rain came through, and the wind was severe. One winter night, the rooms of the monastery were completely ruined. The monks' quarters were damaged and rain and hail covered the floor, making an intolerable situation. A white-haired old monk had to wipe the snow off the top of his head. The old monk, whose eyebrows had grown long, seemed to gather together all the furrows of his large, sad forehead in the face of this difficulty. When the other monks saw him, they too felt justified in feeling sad, and they were not able to do zazen. A monk wanted to rebuild the monastery, but Pai-yün rejected the plan. "Our great teacher, Shakyamuni, said that all things are impermanent. Even the high peaks and deep valleys change. All things are just like thoughts, so how can they satisfy? And it is just so. Ancient worthies practiced on the ground under trees. This is an excellent custom of ancient times. They are the exploits of ancient wise men. When we look back on the practices of the five ancestors, our own practices do not equal theirs. The time when one is able to practice is a mere forty or fifty years. Who has time to build a splendid new building?" Consequently, he paid no attention to the monk's request.

The next day, Fa-yen went to the Dharma hall and spoke to the monks. "When he first went to Mount Yang-ch'i, the rafters and walls were shabby and the beds were wrapped in jewel-like snow, the cold wind shriveled his head, and he sighed in the night, but he recalled that the Buddha had carried out his own practice beneath trees and on rocks." Consequently, Pai-yün Shou-tuan did not approve rebuilding the monks' hall. However, in spite of this, all those under the heavens who wished to practice wanted to be included among his disciples. It is delightful that so many people aspired so deeply to practice the Way. You should therefore inscribe these words on the very organs of your body [literally "on your livers"].

Zen Master Fa-yen once said, "Practice does not transcend thought; thought does not transcend words." You should give these words serious consideration. "Day and night think of it, morning and evening do it" does not mean that you should be restless, as if you were being blown about by the winds of the north, east, south, and west.

The palaces of Japan's emperor and courtiers are simple dwellings thatched with miscanthus; they are not at all splendid palaces. How much less should those who have made their home departure and study the Buddha Way peacefully live in fine houses! Those who have acquired fine dwellings are leading lives of error; those who are pure are rare indeed. It is a different matter if they were owned originally, but you should not try to obtain such a dwelling. The ancient worthies lived in grass-thatched or miscanthus-thatched houses, and that is all they wanted. These are excellent facts. The Ch'in Emperor Hsiang Shih-tzu says in his *Shih-tzu*, "When you look at the conduct of the Yellow Emperor, look at his combined palace. When you want to look at the conduct of Yao and Shun, look at their palaces. The palace from which the Yellow Emperor ruled the country was thatched with grass and was called the combined palace. The palace from which Yao and Shun ruled the country was thatched with grass, and this was called a palace." O disciples, you must understand that these palaces were both thatched with grass. When we compare ourselves now with the Yellow Emperor or Yao and Shun, we are as far apart as heaven and earth. They made grass-thatched dwellings their palaces; how can those who have left the home life live in fine houses and halls? Indeed, it is a disgrace. The ancients lived beneath trees and in forests, and this included both home dwellers and monks, for both desired to live this way. The Yellow Emperor was the disciple of the Taoist master Kuang-ch'eng, who lived among the crags of the mountains called K'ung-t'ung. These days, many of the emperors and their retainers in Sung China transmit this excellent spirit. Consequently, if ordinary people live in this manner, how can those who have made their home departure be any less? How can they be more impure than ordinary people?

Many of those who have been discussed up to this point received help from divine beings, but after the ancestors acquired the great enlightenment, divine beings and spirits lost the power that allowed them to associate with the masters. You should understand this clearly. When these divine beings and spirits conform to the activities of the ancestors, they can associate with them. However, once the masters have become enlightened and go beyond divine beings and spirits, there is no longer any means by which these spirits can see them clearly and they cannot approach them.

Concerning this, Nan-ch'üan said, "This old monk has no power of practice, and so he is easily seen by spirits." You should understand that being seen by these spirits is a result of having no power to practice. It is told that a temple guardian spirit who took the form of a servant in the T'ien-lung Monastery said once, "I have heard that Chief Priest Cheng-chio has lived on this mountain for more than ten years, but whenever I go to where he lives and try to see him, I cannot see him even if he is right in front of me." Truly, non-Buddhists and spirits not being able to see a person enlightened in that chief priest's way is a fine example of the heritage of the ancestors.

This T'ien-lung Monastery was originally a small monastery. While Cheng-chio lived there as chief priest, the Taoist sanctuary and Taoist nuns' monastery were removed and it became the present day Ching-te Monastery. When the master died, and the censor Wang Po-hsiang recorded the master's work, some people said, "The Zen master got rid of the monasteries that taught the teachings of the Taoists, so you should record the place as T'ien-lung Monastery" [i.e., "Heavenly Dragon Monastery"]. To this, the censor replied, "This is not right. It has nothing to do with the merits of the Buddhist priests." Many people praised the censor for this.

You should understand that this sort of thing should be considered a victory for ordinary people, not merits for the Buddhist priesthood. In general, after priests have entered the Buddha Way, they clearly transcend the divine beings and humans of the three worlds. You should deeply comprehend the fact that monks are not utilized by the world or seen by the world. You should thoroughly understand that the activities of body, speech, and mind, and such things as Buddhas and ordinary beings, delusion and enlightenment, and so forth, all come from your own minds.

The merits of the continuous practice of the Buddhas and ancestors are, of course, a great effort made for the sake of gods and humans, but you still do not understand that gods and humans are helped by the continuous practice of the Buddhas and ancestors.

When you now attempt to practice continuously the great Way of the Buddhas and ancestors, it is not at all a question of large or small, or bright or stupid. Just always reject fame and fortune and do not be bound by inner and outer conditions. Don't idle away the time needed for practice, but rather practice in the spirit of a person trying to extinguish a blaze in his hair. Do not sit and wait for enlightenment, for great enlightenment is to be found in everyday activities such as eating or drinking tea. Also, do not wish to transcend enlightenment, for the transcending of enlightenment is truly the jewel in the topknot. The person who lives in his old home should leave it; the person who has thoughts and desires should get rid of them. The famous person should abandon fame, and the person who has benefited materially should get rid of his goods. The person with fields and gardens should part with them, and the person with a family should leave it. You should renounce them even if you do not possess them. What should be clear in this matter is the principle of being free from them whether you have them or not. That is the continuous practice of being free from everything, whatever it is. Simply making an earnest effort to practice continuously and to get rid of fame and fortune is the continuous practice of making the life of the Buddha eternal. This present continuous practice is nothing other than just that, just committing oneself to continuous practice for no other reason than to practice continuously. Therefore, you should love and respect this mind and body that support continuous practice.

The Zen master Ta-tz'u Huan-chung said, "It is better to walk one foot than to talk ten feet; it is better to move one inch than to talk one foot." In a way, this is admonishing people of the present who are negligent about continuous practice and forget those things that are part of the Buddha Way, but it is not saying that it is wrong to "talk ten feet." It simply says that one foot of real effort is by far more important than talking ten feet. How could it be merely a question of the difference between one foot and ten feet? It is by far easier to talk about the difference between Mount Sumeru and a grain of sesame. However, Mount Sumeru is the whole of Mount Sumeru, and the sesame seed is the whole of the sesame seed. The greatness of continuous practice is like that. These words are not just Huan-chung's words; they are words that transcend words.

The Zen master Tung-shan Wu-pen said, "Speak what cannot be performed; do what cannot be spoken." This was this great priest's Way. Its true meaning is that action thoroughly pervades speech, and speech thoroughly pervades action. A whole day of speaking is a whole day of action. This is practicing what cannot be practiced and speaking what cannot be spoken.

The great master Hung-chüeh of Mount Yün-chü explained with regard to Tung-shan's statement, "When one speaks, there is no action, and when one acts, there is no speech." This does not mean that there is no speech or no action. "Speaking" means not leaving the Zen monastery for your whole life. "Action" means speaking by means of silence, as seen in the story of a certain monk who washed his head and went before Hsüeh-feng.[90] Do not be negligent about this.

Something excellent has been transmitted from ancient times by the Buddhas: "Even if a person lives for a hundred years, if he does not come to know himself as a Buddha, he is not the equal of someone who lives for only one day and is able to thoroughly comprehend it." This was not said by just one Buddha or two Buddhas; it has been taught by all the Buddhas and has been put into practice by all the Buddhas. Within the eternal round of life and death, the single day of continuous practice is the bright jewel in the topknot. It is the true self that I share [literally, "It is the ancient mirror that has the same life and death as I do."]. It is a day to be joyously appreciated. Continuous practice is delight by virtue of the power of continuous practice. If the power of continuous practice is still insufficient, and you do not inherit the bone and marrow of all the Buddhas, you will not hold the bodies and minds of all the Buddhas in high esteem, and you will not rejoice at seeing all the faces of the Buddhas. The enlightenment of all the Buddhas does not go away, it goes according to the suchness of things, and it comes according to the suchness of things. Although it does not come, we shall still inherit it by means of this one day of continuous effort.

Therefore, one day should be valued and respected. A hundred years idly lived is a hundred years to be regretted. It is a shambles to be deplored. However, though you are wastefully enslaved to a hundred years of just running about here and there, if you involve yourself in continuous practice for just one day, you not only practice for a hundred years of this one lifetime, but you also help the hundred years of the next lifetime. This life of one day is a life to rejoice in. Because of this, even though you live for just one day, if you can be awakened to the truth, that one day is vastly superior to an eternal life. Therefore, people who are not yet enlightened should not waste this one day. This one day is a priceless jewel that we should value highly. You cannot compare it even with a huge jewel. Do not replace it even with a dragon's jewel. The ancient wise men valued this one day even more than their own lives. Surely that is something to think about. The dragon's jewel can be sought; the huge jewel may be right in your hand. However, if this one day in the lifetime of a hundred years is lost, will you ever get your hands on it again? Whatever skillful devices you may employ, there is no example in history of anyone recovering a day that has passed. Wastefully spending a day is wastefully spending time that is ours. For this reason, ancient wise people valued time more than their own bodies or more than their native soil. Spending time wastefully is being seduced by the fame and fortune of this transitory world. Not spending time wastefully is being within the Way; it is activity done for the sake of the Way. As for those who are already enlightened, they will not spend even one day wastefully. They earnestly act for the sake of the Way; they speak for the sake of the Way. Thus, we can understand why none of the Buddhas of the past squandered even a single day of practice. You must always keep this in mind. Think of this when you sit beside a bright window, leisurely spending a spring day. Do not forget it while you sit in a thatched house on a quiet, solitary, rainy night. Is it the light and dark that rob us of practice? They do not steal just a day. They pilfer away the merit of many ages to come. What enmity exists between us and the light and shade? Truly it is a bitter thing, but our neglect of practice is something we should blame ourselves for, though we do not reproach ourselves. The Buddhas and ancestors were not without thoughts and desires, but they got rid of them. The Buddhas and ancestors were not above ordinary conditions either, but they freed themselves from them. Though we may somewhat regret those conditions that are found within and without us, we do not utterly regret them. Consequently, if we do not abandon thoughts and desires, they will abandon us. If you very much regret your thoughts and desires, get rid of them. Truly, regretting thoughts and desires very much means getting rid of them.

Chief Priest Huai-jang, who was the Zen master Ta-hui of Nan-yueh, practiced at Mount Ts'ao-ch'i, where for fifteen years he served the sixth [Chinese] ancestor. He inherited the Way in the manner in which water is transferred from one bucket to another. The practice of predecessors such as these should be highly respected. There must have been many things among those fifteen autumns of varied activity that may trouble us. However, the fact that he did zazen and earnestly learned the Way is now a mirror for those who continue after him. There were no coals in the stove in the winter, and on autumn nights when he had no lamp, he faced the bright window and did zazen, and though this has not been widely known, it was unconditioned, absolute learning. We should consider it to be the essence of continuous practice.

Generally speaking, if we cease being attached in our hearts to fame and fortune, daily things such as eating or drinking tea become the accumulation of continuous practice. Do not forget this. Zen Master Huai-jang's statement, "Though you may talk about the realm of great enlightenment, words cannot reveal reality, for language is just concepts. The realm of great enlightenment is real, it is experience. That realm that was acquired for the first time after eight years of continuous practice [by Shakyamuni]," is a rare thing in either the past or the present. But it is the continuous practice that both the wise and the ignorant should aspire to.

When the Zen master Chih-hsien was practicing with Ta-wei, he tried to say something that would indicate his enlightenment, but he could not say a single word. This grieved him, and he burned up all his books and spent several years as a serving-monk in the monks' hall. Later, he climbed Mount Wu-tang and sought the whereabouts of Nan-yang Hui-chung. There, he built a hermitage of grass, cut his connections with the world, and lived a peaceful life. One day, when he was sweeping the path, a stone flew and struck bamboo, and when he heard the sound, he was immediately enlightened. Later, he became head monk at Hsiang-yen Monastery, and all he ever owned was one bowl and one set of robes, and he never exchanged them for new ones while he was head monk. With no one for companions except the strange rocks and a stream of clear water, he lived an inconspicuous life in tranquillity. It is said that once he entered the mountains, he never again came down. The traces of this continuous practice are transmitted to this day at Wu-tang Monastery.

The great master Hui-chao of Lin-chi Monastery was the legitimate heir of Huang-po, and he spent three years as Huang-po's disciple. He followed the Way single-mindedly and followed the teaching of Ch'en-tao Monastery in Mu-chou. Three times he asked Huang-po about the great meaning of the Buddhadharma and its fundamental ideas, and altogether he was thrashed sixty times with the *keisaku*. He burned with a fiery spirit for seeking the Way. Then he visited Kao-an Ta-yü and had a great satori, but it was really due to the two Zen masters, Huang-po and Ta-yü. It has been said that the best of the ancestors were Lin-chi and Te-shan, but how can Te-shan be put in the same category with Lin-chi? Truly, the Zen man Lin-chi was without an equal in the whole crowd. But the Zen world of that time was more preeminent than that of today. It is said that they practiced earnestly and that they were preeminent in continuous practice, but though we may attempt to resolve the question of the extent of their continuous practice, we ought not bother to do it.

When Lin-chi was at Mount Huang-po, while he was planting some cedars and pines one day with the monk Huang-po, Huang-po asked him, "Why on earth are we planting so many trees right here in this deep valley?" Lin-chi answered, "First, to improve the scenery around the monastery. Second, to serve as a guide for those who come after us." Now, Lin-chi's idea was that ordinary events are not imitations. He wanted to actively show the original face in continuous practice and to be a guidemarker for the continuous practice of others, and crossing swords with Huang-po was a sign he raised. Lin-chi held up a hoe before Huang-po's face and twice struck the ground forcefully with it. At this, Huang-po just raised his staff. "I have raised my staff thus, but haven't you already tasted the thirty blows?" Lin-chi made a sighing sound but remained silent. "My teaching will become widely known in the world in your time," concluded Huang-po.

Therefore, you should understand that when he planted trees even after acquiring the Way, Lin-chi personally held the hoe in his own hands. Huang-po was not mistaken when he said that his teaching would flourish in the world in Lin-chi's time because of this. These old precedents of people who practiced the Way by planting pines are still being transmitted today. Huang-po and Lin-chi both planted trees. During Huang-po's time, he left all the monks who followed him and became involved in the general work at Ta-an Monastery, where his continuous practice consisted of sweeping out all the rooms. He swept the Buddha hall and Dharma hall. But it was not continuous practice done for the sake of sweeping out the mind, nor was it continuous practice performed in order to cleanse the light of the Buddha. It was continuous practice done for the sake of continuous practice. It was about this time that he met the government official P'ei-hsui, who became Huang-po's disciple.

Emperor Hsüan-tsung was the second son of Emperor Hsien-tung. He was intelligent and wise from the time he was small. He loved to sit in the lotus position. While he was at the palace, he always did zazen. Mu-tsung was his elder brother. When Mu-tsung ascended the throne, Hsüan-tsung would playfully sit on the throne and pretend to greet the officials after the early-morning affairs of state had been concluded. When the court officials saw him do this, they thought he was crazy, and they told Mu-tsung about it. He went to see for himself and praised Hsüan-tsung: "My brother is the superior heir in this family." At the time, Hsüan-tsung was only thirteen years old.

In 814, Mu-tsung died. Mu-tsung had three sons: Ching-tsung, Wen-tsung, and Wu-tsung. Ching-tsung died after occupying his father's throne for only three years. Wen-tsung is said to have been on the throne for only one year and was forced to abdicate by close associates. So Wu-tsung became Emperor and Hsüan-tsung did not, and Hsüan-tsung stayed in his nephew's country. Wu-tsung always called him his "crazy uncle." Wu-tsung was emperor from 841 to 846. He was the one who persecuted Buddhism at that time.

One time, Wu-tsung called his uncle and, in order to punish him for getting up on his father's throne as a boy, hit him a strong blow. Afterward, he revived him in the garden by urinating on him. Hsüan-tsung thereupon left the land of his father, shaved his head, and became a novice monk under Zen Master Chih-hsien. However, he had not yet taken the complete precepts of the monk. He traveled about in many prefectures with Chih-hsien, and finally they arrived at Mount Lu. Chih-hsien, taking a waterfall as his theme, composed this verse:

> Dragon waters bore into the cliffs and scrape away the rocks,
> But they do not ever hate their labor.
> When you see it from afar,
> You fully know how high the dragon's mouth is.

He was testing the novice monk with this verse in an attempt to see what kind of person he was. The novice continued the verse:

> Can the water in the valleys ever stop and rest?
> When the water finally reaches the sea, it becomes great waves.

When Chih-hsien heard these lines, he knew the novice monk was not an ordinary person.

Afterward, Hsüan-tsung became the disciple of the National Teacher Yen-kuan Ch'i-an of Hang-chou, who made him a secretary-scribe. Zen Master Huang-po was made Yen-kuan's chief priest at that time. Consequently, Hsüan-tsung and Huang-po sat side by side in the meditation hall. Once, when Huang-po went to the Buddha hall and bowed before the Buddha, Hsüan-tsung came and asked him, "Since the Buddhadharma is an unobtainable Dharma that cannot be sought, and you cannot seek the Buddha, Dharma, and Sangha, why do you do this bowing?" When spoken to in this manner, Huang-po slapped the secretary with his palm and remarked gently, "I bow just because one cannot seek the Buddha, Dharma, and Sangha." To this, Hsüan-tsung answered, "Too crude." Huang-po countered this with, "There isn't a single thing within this body that seeks the Three Jewels, so how can it speak either crudely or subtly?" And once more he slapped Hsüan-tsung with the palm of his hand. Hsüan-tsung left.

After Emperor Wu died, this secretary left the priesthood and became emperor. He repealed Wu-tsung's proclamation, which caused the persecution of Buddhism, and became its protector. While he was on the throne, he always valued zazen. When he was no longer emperor, he left his father's land again and visited the distant valleys of Mount Lu, where he earnestly did zazen. It is said that after he left the throne, he did zazen day and night. Truly, with his father dead, brothers dead, mistreated by his nephew, and so on, he seemed to be in a pitiful situation. However, his diligence in the Buddha Way was as solid as diamond, and he never neglected practice. Truly, all this is a splendid historical fact concerning continuous practice the likes of which are rarely encountered.

As soon as the great master Hsüeh-feng Chen-chüeh, who was the chief priest I-ts'un, had aroused the thought of enlightenment, he began to join the groups of disciples at Zen monasteries in all localities, where he would serve as the monk in charge of eating regulations. He always carried a large wooden spoon around with him. Thus, he wandered around to various monasteries in all the localities, where he would continue his own practice by serving the monks in the capacity of *tien-ts'o* [head cook; *tenzō* in Japanese]. Whether pressed with work or at his leisure time, he never disliked where he was, and he never forgot to do zazen day and night. Up to the time he founded the training hall at Mount Hsüeh-feng, he did not forget to share his life and death with zazen. While he was an itinerant priest, he visited Tung-shan Liang-chieh nine different times, and he visited T'ou-tzu Ta-t'ung three times—truly a rare seeker of the Way in this world.

In promoting the noble majesty of continuous practice among people, many people in the present time praise the exalted continuous practice of Hsüeh-feng. Even though the beginning of the

continuous practice

151

search for the Way by Hsüeh-feng is no different from that of other people, the sharpness of his prajñā insight and will make him far removed from all others. It was continuous practice that enabled him to do it. Disciples today ought to penetrate the depths of Hsüeh-feng's majestic continuous practice. When we quietly look back on his courage and diligence in practicing in all those places, truly, we understand that those things were the superb practice that is now being transmitted.

When you aspire to train under the enlightened masters, it is most difficult to catch any information you may be given when you inquire individually. There are not just twenty or thirty; there are hundreds and thousands of people making inquiry. Because you are studying Buddhism and seeking enlightenment under various masters, when you try out all their teachings, the sun will set and the day will completely end. Or else when the master addresses the students, they may have no talent and are utterly indifferent to the teaching. On the other hand, they may have talent, but the teacher concludes his remarks. It is indeed a rare occurrence, if you are a younger person or have started to practice late in life, to be able to sit on the far end of the sitting platform and hear the old-timers clap their hands and laugh to hear the Dharma taught. There are those who enter the training hall and those who do not, those who are touched by the master's teaching and acquire the Way, and those who do not. Days and nights pass faster than an arrow; the body is more delicate than the dew on the grass. Even though there is a teacher, we get trapped by circumstances, and it is a pity we are unable to train. It is also a pity that even though we try to train, we cannot find a teacher. I have seen this situation with my own eyes.

The great masters possess the insight that enables them to know whether a person is wise or unwise, but it is indeed rare that diligent disciples find a happy situation near a great teacher. Long ago, when Hsüeh-feng climbed Mount Lu nine times and went to T'ou-tzu three times, he surely put up with much trouble and discomfort. You should sympathize with this commitment to continuous practice, and you should pity those who do not practice continuously with their very bodies.

Kajō

"EVERYDAY LIFE"

Among the Buddha ancestors, drinking tea and eating rice is everyday life. This matter of drinking tea and eating rice has been transmitted over a long period of time [since the days of the Buddha], and it is now manifested in everyday life. Therefore, this tea drinking and rice eating of the ancestors has been transmitted to the present time as the everyday life of the ancestors.

The priest Tao-k'ai of Mount Ta-yang asked his teacher, the Zen master T'ou-tzu, "Are the words that the ancestors use for teaching the same as their daily life of drinking tea and eating rice? Are there any other words different from these which are used to teach people?" T'ou-tzu replied, "Well, let me ask you, since this land is governed by the decrees of the emperor, does he have any need to borrow power from the Hsia emperor Yü of ancient times, or from the Yin emperor T'ang, or from Yao and Shun?" Tao-k'ai started to speak, but T'ou-tu covered his mouth with his *hossu* [fly whisk] and said, "When you came here to ask that, you should have received thirty blows." Hearing this, Tao-k'ai experienced satori. He bowed and started to leave. T'ou-tzu called after him, "Tao-k'ai, come here a moment." But Tao-k'ai would not look back. Once, later, T'ou-tzu asked him, "Did you attain the realm of satori?" But Tao-k'ai covered his ears and left.

It is clear that you yourselves must guard and maintain these words of the ancestors that are their daily life of drinking tea and eating rice. The plain tea and light food of everyday life are the deep meaning of the Buddha's teaching and the instructions of the ancestors. The ancestors prepare tea and rice, and tea and rice maintain the ancestors. However, they do not rely on any other power than that of drinking tea and eating rice. They just do not waste the powers of Buddha ancestors that they have within them.

You must make a great effort and penetrate T'ou-tzu's question, "Does he have any need to borrow the power of the Hsia emperor Yü of ancient times, or of the Yin emperor T'ang, or of Yao and Shun?" On the other hand, you should also penetrate the inner meaning of Tao-k'ai's question of whether the ancestors have any other words of instruction apart from eating rice and drinking tea, and then you must transcend this inner meaning. You should really carefully examine whether you have transcended either the affirmation or negation of this borrowing.

The Zen master Shih-t'ou Wu-chi of Mount Nan-yüeh said, "I have built this grass hermitage here, and I do not have a single thing of value. After I have eaten, if I am sleepy I leisurely take a nap." Now, though the words of instruction come and go, this "after I have eaten" means that Shih-t'ou has eaten his fill of the ancestors' words. Not yet having eaten is the same as not being satisfied. However, this principle called "after I have eaten I leisurely take a nap" is manifested before eating, during eating, and after eating. It is mistaken to think that after eating one does not eat rice or drink tea. To proceed in this way is appropriate study.

My teacher, the old Buddha [Ju-ching], once said to the monks, "According to an ancient kōan, a monk once asked Pai-chang, 'What is the very best thing of all?' Pai-chang answered, 'Doing zazen alone on top of Ta-hsiung Peak.' You monks should not be nonplussed by this. Furthermore, you should surpass Pai-chang when you sit. If someone were to ask me now what the very best thing of all is, I would say, there is something that is extremely excellent, and do you know what in the world it is? Eating rice with the begging bowl I brought to Mount T'ien-lung from Ching-tz'u Monastery." There is surely something very excellent in the daily lives of the ancestors, and it is "doing zazen alone on Ta-hsiung Peak." The matter of surpassing Pai-chang is also the very best thing. However, there is something that is even better than these, and that is eating rice with the begging bowl I brought to Mount T'ien-lung from Ching-tz'u

Monastery. The very best thing is that everything is just eating rice and drinking tea. However, doing zazen alone on Ta-hsiung Peak is the same as eating rice and drinking tea. The begging bowl has for its function eating rice, and the function of eating rice is the begging bowl. For this reason, the begging bowl of Ching-tz'u Monastery is the same as eating rice at Mount T'ien-lung. When you have had all the rice you can eat, you then know what rice is; when once you have eaten rice, you are satisfied. Once you have come to know what rice is, then you eat as much as you wish; and once you are satisfied, you eat rice again. Just what is this begging bowl? I do not think that it is just something made of wood, nor is it something made of black lacquer, nor something made of iron. It has no bottom and no opening. It can swallow the universe in a single mouthful, and the whole universe receives it with [palms together in] *gasshō*.

Another time my teacher, the old Buddha, said in a Dharma talk at the Ching-tu Hall in Shui-yen Monastery in T'ai country, "When hungry, eat; when tired, sleep. The hearth flames will fill the sky." "When hungry" means the lives of those who have eaten rice. Those who have not yet eaten rice are the people who are not hungry yet. However, you should understand that we whose hunger is our daily life must affirm that it is ourselves who have eaten rice. "Tired" means tiredness within tiredness. It is tiredness that includes the totality of tiredness. For this reason, it is this present moment when the life of the whole body [and mind] is completely unified with the whole body. "Sleep" means sleeping with the eyes of the Buddha, the eyes of the Dharma, the eyes of insight, the eyes of the ancestors, and the eyes of round pillars and lanterns.

My teacher, the old Buddha, once went from Shui-yen Monastery in T'ai country at the request of Ching-tz'u Monastery, in Lien-an, and before leaving he spoke in the Dharma hall:

For half a year I ate the rice of Shui-yen Monastery and always
    did zazen on Mang Peak.
Once while I sat, the misty clouds gathered, piling up one on top
    of the other.
Thunder shook the earth, and the sky grew dark;
In the capital, the spring colors, the red of apricot blossoms.

The ancestors who teach and convert in place of the Buddha do so by doing zazen on Mang Peak and eating rice. The intensive study of the Buddha's compassion and life is revealed in this life of eating rice. Doing zazen on Mang Peak for half a year is the same as "eating rice." We do not know how deeply piled up are the misty clouds that are dispersed by zazen; even though thunder shakes the whole earth, it is just the spring color of apricot blossoms turning deep scarlet. "Capital" means the orderliness of the scarlet blossoms. The "thusness" of these blossoms is just eating rice. "Mang Peak" is the name of a mountain near Shui-yen Monastery.

One time at Shui-yen Monastery, my old teacher said to the assembled monks, "The golden, wonderful body [of the Buddha] is just the daily life of wearing robes and eating rice, and for that reason, I bow to you. Each day I arise in the morning with this golden form and each night I retire with it. Ha! The preaching of the wonderful Dharma for forty-nine years by the Buddha was uncouth. How offensive of him to hold up the flower and thereby deceive himself." You must understand that the wonderful golden body of the Buddha is the same as wearing robes and eating rice. Wearing clothes and eating rice is the wonderful golden body. This is the way one experiences the Buddha Way. Therefore, my master made a bow before the monks. When I eat rice, you also bow to that eating of rice. How much better had the Buddha not held up the flower and deceived himself.

The Zen master Yüan-chih of Ch'ang-ching Hall, in Fu country, once addressed the monks in the Dharma hall: "For thirty years I lived on Mount Wei, and during that time I ate the monastery's rice and gave it back in the latrine. I did not learn the Zen of Master Wei-shan. All I did was raise an ox. When he wandered from the path into the grass, I pulled him back; when he ran amuck in someone's garden, I chastised him with a whip. Now he has been tame for some time. Unfortunately he used to pay too much attention to what people said, but now, however, he has become a pure white domesticated ox. He is always right in front of me wherever I am, dazzling white all day long, and even if I try to drive him away, he will not go." We should pay careful attention to this story. The thirty years of arduous effort with the ancestor [Wei-shan] consisted of eating rice, and there was no other consideration. When you realize the meaning of this life of eating rice, you will also understand the deep meaning of raising the ox.

The great master Chao-chou Chen-chi once asked a new monk, "Have you ever been here before?" "Yes, I have," replied the monk. Chao-chou then said, "Then please have some tea before you leave." Chao-chou asked another monk, "Have you ever been here before?" The monk replied, "No, I have not." "Well then," said Chao-chou, "please have some tea before you leave." An assistant of the monastery asked Chao-chou, "Why did you say 'Please have some tea before you leave' to both the monk who had been here before and the monk who had not?" Chao-chou called to the assistant, "O assistant!" "Yes," responded the monk. "Please have some tea before you leave," said Chao-chou. The "here" of this story is neither the head nor the nostrils of the ancestors, nor has it any connection with Chao-chou. Because we transcend "here," we may say, "Yes, I have been here before," or, "No, I have not been here before." Because you contain within you the place of suchness, you may continue to speak of "have been here" and "not been here." Therefore, Ju-ching said, "What person drenched in wine in a gaudily painted mansion can ever taste Chao-chou's tea when they meet?" The everyday life of the ancestors is nothing but drinking tea and eating rice.

Notes

1. *The Platform Sutra of the Sixth Ancestor,* trans. Philip B. Yampolsky (New York: Columbia University Press, 1967), p. 135.

2. *Bendōwa,* trans. Norman Waddell and Abe Masao, in *Eastern Buddhist,* 6, no. 1 (1973), p. 128.

3. *Ibid.,* p. 129.

4. *Bendōwa,* in *Dōgen shū (Nihon no shisō,* vol. 2), ed. Tamaki Koshirō (Tokyo: Chikuma Shobo, 1969), p. 130.

5. *Shōji,* trans. Norman Waddell and Abe Masao, in *Eastern Buddhist,* 5, no. 1 (1972), pp. 79–80.

6. *Genjō kōan,* trans. Taizan Maezumi Roshi and Francis Cook (Los Angeles: Zen Center of Los Angeles Press, 1977), p. 2. This is a revision of the translation by Chōtan Aitken Roshi and Tanahashi Kazuaki.

7. *The Platform Sutra of the Sixth Ancestor,* p. 140.

8. *Genjō kōan.* See note 6 above.

9. Quoted by Akiyama Hanji in *Dōgen no kenkyū* (Tokyo: Reimei Shobo, 1965), p. 248.

10. *Hotsu mujō shin,* in Okada Gihō, *Shōbōgenzō shisō taikei* vol. 6 (Tokyo: Hosei University Press), p. 77.

11. *Gakudō yōjinshū,* in Yamaguchi Shinju, "Dōgen Zenji ni okeru shingyō no Mondai," *Indogaku bukkyōgaku kenkyū,* 13, no. 1 (1965), p. 83.

12. *Shōbōgenzō shisō taikei,* vol. 6, p. 15.

13. *Kie sambō,* in *Shōbōgenzō shisō taikei,* vol. 6, p. 176.

14. *Kesa kudoku,* in *Dōgen shū,* pp. 270–71.

15. *Ibid.*, p. 276.

16. *Ibid.*, p. 289. This is recited daily in the *zendō*.

17. *Bendōwa,* in *Dōgen shū,* p. 104.

18. Akiyama Hanji and Okada Gihō, among other Japanese scholars, highlight Dōgen's Zen as a Buddhism of faith. See Akiyama, *Dōgen no kenkyū,* p. 325, and Okada, *Shōbōgenzō shisō taikei,* vol. 6, p. 17.

19. *A Primer of Sōtō Zen (Shōbōgenzō Zuimonki),* trans. Masunaga Reihō (Honolulu: East-West Center Press, 1971), p. 56.

20. Karako Shajo, "My Faith in Shikan-taza," unpublished typescript, n.d.

21. *Bendōwa,* in *Dōgen shū,* p. 130.

22. *Hotsu bodai shin,* quoted by Okada Gihō, in *Shōbōgenzō shisō taikei* (Tokyo: Hosei University Press), vol. 6, p. 116.

23. *Entering the Path of Enlightenment: The Bodhicāryāvatāra of the Buddhist Poet Śantideva,* trans. Marion L. Matics (New York: MacMillan Co., 1970).

24. *A Primer of Sōtō Zen (Shōbōgenzō Zuimonki),* trans. Masunaga Reihō, p. 62.

25. *Fukan zazengi,* in *Dōgen shū,* p. 55.

26. *Hotsu bodai shin,* in *Shōbōgenzō shisō taikei* vol. 6, p. 113.

27. *The Laṅkāvatāra Sūtra,* trans. Daisetz T. Suzuki (London: Routledge and Kegan Paul, 1932), p. 184. "Mahāmati, when the Bodhisattvas face and perceive the happiness of the samādhi of perfect tranquillization, they are moved with the feeling of love and sympathy owing to their original vows, and they become aware of the part they are to perform as regard the [ten] inexhaustible vows. Thus, they do not enter Nirvana. But the fact is that they are already in Nirvana, because in them there is no arising of discrimination."

28. *Hotsu bodai shin,* in *Shōbōgenzō shisō taikei* vol. 6, p. 118.

29. *Ibid.,* p. 119.

30. *Hotsu mujō shin,* in *Zenyaku shōbōgenzō,* vol. 3, trans. Nakamura Sōichi (Tokyo: Seishin Shobo, 1972–73), p. 173.

31. Shibayama Zenkei, *Zen Comments on The Mumonkan* (New York: Harper and Row, 1976), p. 33.

32. An allusion to the methods of the so-called Northern school of Zen taught by Shen-hsiu, competitor with Hui-neng for the title of sixth ancestor. The mind was conceived as being like a bright mirror that reflects everything as long as it is kept immaculate, which is to say, free of discriminating thought. Hui-neng said that there is no mirror and therefore nothing to be defiled.

33. A *hossu* is a whisk made of horse- or yak-tail hairs and was carried by the Zen priests as a symbol of rank. The raising or lowering of the *hossu* was often used by Zen masters as a teaching device, as were all the other devices such as shouting, hitting, and so on.

34. The seal of the Buddha is Buddha mind, which is said to be transmitted by the Zen tradition.

35. These are different methods of meditation or different methods of training in general.

36. There is a very old story of several blind men examining an elephant by touch and trying to decide what the elephant is like. Because each touches only one part of the elephant, each has a partial and therefore inadequate idea of what an elephant is. The second reference is to a famous artist who specialized in painting dragons. One day a real dragon flew into his room and the artist did not know what it was.

37. A reference to the story in which Hui-k'o cut off one of his arms and presented it to Bodhidharma in order to demonstrate his sincerity in seeking the Dharma. Dōgen mentions this episode several times in *Shōbōgenzō,* citing Hui-k'o as an example of the very strong determination required by one who seeks the Dharma. Hui-k'o eventually received the Dharma transmission from Bodhidharma, becoming the second Chinese Zen ancestor.

38. A well-known poet who lived during the Sung Dynasty in China.

39. *Nagas* are water deities said to guard Buddhist scriptures.

40. The commentaries give the source of this quotation as the *Ta chih tu lun,* a lengthy commentary on the *Prajñāpāramitā Sūtra.*

41. From the *Lotus Sutra,* in the chapter named "Easy Practice."

42. This means that Buddha, living beings, and insentient things are all the One Mind.

43. Allusions to two episodes in the *Lotus Sutra* and *Ta chih tu lun* respectively. The story of the drunken Brahmin who received the precepts

and made his home departure while drunk is told in Dōgen's *Shukke* ("Home Departure"). There, he cites the thirteenth volume of the *Ta chih tu lun* as his source.

44. From the *Mahāvibhāsā, Taishō,* no. 1545.

45. These are allusions to two well-known enlightenment experiences. When Ling-yuan was wandering in the mountains, he unexpectedly came upon a place where some people were living, and when he saw the peach blossoms, he became enlightened. The second case is that of Hsiang-yen Chih-hsien, who was sweeping the path of his hermitage and became enlightened when he heard the sound of a pebble striking a bamboo. Both incidents are discussed in Dōgen's *Keisei sanshoku* ("The sounds of the valley streams and the forms of the mountains").

46. Both incidents are derived from the *Lotus Sutra.*

47. Either "unconditioned," or "unmade," which really mean the same, both being translations of the Sanskrit *asamskrita.*

48. This also means "unconditioned," but to avoid repetition of the term used above, I have adopted the Taoist meaning of "non-self-assertive." It refers to an act that is not performed for self-gratification.

49. Sometimes translated as "real-mark," or "true-mark" (Richard Robinson and others), and sometimes, as here, "the revelation of ultimate reality." It is the mark that all things possess, consisting of being just what they are in themselves. A synonym would be "suchness" or "isness," sometimes used as a translation of the Sanskrit *tathatā.*

50. Dharma-state *(hō-i):* this refers to the specific temporal and spacial location of what we may term as "event"; i.e., something concrete taking place. This event is *just that* and nothing else, containing within itself the totality of a specific experience, with no limiting or partial elements. "Thus the act of eating, for example, is viewed as the absolute given, self-sufficient in itself; it is the *kōan* realized in life *(Genjōkōan)."* Hee-jin Kim, *Dōgen Kigen: Mystical Realist* (University of Arizona Press, 1975), p. 200.

51. References to stories about the Zen masters Tung-shan and Hui-neng. The reference to Hui-neng concerns his treading in the stone mortar while pounding rice, even though he had already acquired the Dharma.

52. The *Ch'an yüan ch'ing kuei* is a well known list of monastic regulations of Chinese origin (*ch'ing kuei* are monastic regulations, which the Japanese call *shingi*), and is one of several such documents. *Ch'ing kuei*

give detailed instructions for the living of the monastic life, including eating, bathing, interrelations between superiors and inferiors, use of the toilets and libraries, and so on. This *ch'ing kuei* was brought to Japan by Dōgen. It is said to be related in spirit to the *Pai-chang ch'ing kuei,* the first of its kind in Chinese Zen.

53. Mahākāshyapa was the spiritual successor of Shakyamuni, according to the Zen lineage charts.

54. *The Large Sutra on the Perfection of Wisdom* is the *Pañcaviṃśatisāhas-rikā prajñāpāramitā sūtra,* the best known of the longer versions of this literature.

55. A lengthy commentary on the above sutra, ascribed to Nāgārjuna but suspected to have been composed by its supposed translator into Chinese, Kumārajīva.

56. The word translated as "marrow" here also means "essence," and I have used both translation terms. The allusion is to the tradition according to which Bodhidharma recognized Hui-k'o's attainment by saying that he would receive his marrow or essence. Two other monks and one nun received Bodhidharma's skin, flesh, and bones.

57. The *mondō* exchange was between Hui-neng and some monks. This is case 29 in the collection of kōans named *Mumonkan.*

58. This phrase is my abbreviated translation of "three virtues and ten wisdoms." These are stages of development according to a scheme taught by the Hua-yen school. In all, there are fifty-three stages, the last three comprising stages of Buddhahood. The ten wisdoms are the ten stages just prior to the stages of Buddhahood, comprising stages forty-one through fifty. The three virtues are really thirty stages divided up into three groups and comprise stages eleven through forty. In other words, bodhisattvas in these stages are highly developed in virtue and wisdom.

59. The seven-year-old girl who becomes a Buddha is found in the *Lotus Sutra.* She is identified in the following lines of Dōgen's text.

60. In pre-Mahayana Buddhism, the stage of arhat was considered to be the goal and end of religious practice. The arhat is one who has eliminated all moral and intellectual faults, has ended the round of death and rebirth, understands the four holy truths, and has, in short, completed his or her spiritual training. The Buddha was an arhat as well as being perfectly enlightened.

61. The "four fruits" or "four results" are four stages of spiritual development according to pre-Mahayana Buddhism. In ascending order of
perfection they are: "stream-enterer"; "once-returner" (i.e., one who
will be reborn in human form one more time); "nonreturner" (i.e.,
one who will not be reborn in human form but will attain the stage of
arhat in the world of the celestials); and arhat (see note 60).

62. "Small vehicle" refers to pre-Mahayana Buddhism. It is a pejorative
name for a form of Buddhism that was considered by Mahayana Buddhism to be exclusive and elitist with respect to who could become an
arhat. The small vehicle excluded women in their estimate of who
could achieve spiritual perfection, hence Dōgen's criticism.

63. Dōgen's references to a well-known story in the Zen tradition that is
found in Mumon's commentary on case 28 in the *Mumonkan.* Te-shan
was a well-known lecturer on the *Diamond Sutra.* One day in his travels
he stopped for refreshments. The word in Chinese that we translate as
"refreshment" literally means "to punctuate the mind." The old woman
who sold the refreshments said she would give him refreshments if he
could tell her what mind it is that is punctuated, since the *Diamond Sutra*
says that the past mind is unobtainable, present mind is unobtainable, and
future mind is unobtainable. The learned Te-shan could not answer, so
the old woman threw away the refreshments. Later, in consternation, Te-
shan burned all his commentaries and notes on the *Diamond Sutra.*

64. The term I have translated as "restricted territories" (Jap., *kekkai*) refers
to precincts or areas, including Buddhist temples and monasteries,
which are united or bound to the Dharma. The term literally means
"bound territories" or "fixed territories"; i.e., bound or fixed to the
Dharma. However, Dōgen's criticism centers on the fact that these
places were restricted to all females, whether nuns or laywomen, and I
have tried to capture this in my translation.

65. See note 61.

66. According to Hua-yen Buddhism, the spiritual path consists of fifty-
two stages, of which the last two are aspects of enlightenment. The
fifty-first stage is called "perfect enlightenment" or "uniform enlightenment." The final stage is called "wonderful enlightenment." Dōgen's
point, which follows in the text, is that a seven-year-old girl once
attained this stage. See following note.

67. The seven-year-old girl who became a perfectly enlightened Buddha is
famous in Mahayana Buddhism. The story is told in the *Sadharma-
pundarika Sutra (Lotus Sutra)* in the chapter named "Devadatta."

68. The terms "conditioned" and "nonconditioned" in this passage and later on in the essay are my attempt to translate the terms *p'ien* and *cheng,* both of which are key terms in Tung-shan's well-known "five ranks." The expression *p'ien chung cheng* refers to the first rank, which may be translated as "the nonconditioned within the conditioned." *Cheng chung p'ien,* which is the second rank, means "the conditioned within the nonconditioned." Other terms might be substituted; *cheng* means "correct," "upright," "principle," "true," and so on. *P'ien* means "partial," "inclined," "one-sided," and so on. As contraries, they can also be seen in terms of *li* and *shih,* emptiness and form, the absolute and determined, and so on, and this fundamental Chinese pattern of thinking forms the basis of the discussion in *Shunjū.* A discussion of Tung-shan's "five ranks" may be found in Heinrich Dumoulin's *History of Zen Buddhism,* and in Charles Luk's *Ch'an and Zen Teaching: Second Series.*

69. The "it" referred to here, according to the commentaries, may be either the "five ranks" system, or the problem that forms the substance of the kōan.

70. According to the commentaries, "dry ashes" refers to the vehicle of the srāvakas and pratyekabuddhas, which are referred to by Mahayana Buddhists as the "two vehicles." The reference seems to be to the tendency of the two vehicles to make a sharp distinction between samsara and nirvana, a distinction denied by Mahayana Buddhism in general, and by Dōgen in particular. The important question in this essay is precisely that of "Where is there to be found that place where one is free from birth and death?" Dōgen's comments make it clear that it is this very realm of birth and death.

71. The phrase I have translated here as "a word to change one's mental attitude" is literally "turning word" in Japanese. It is a technical expression in Zen, referring to the appropriate words or expressions uttered by a Zen master in confrontation with a disciple, for the purpose of causing a mental "turning" or transformation. Pai-chang's answer to the old man is an example. Usually in Zen literature, these "turning words" are followed by the statement that the disciple had a satori.

72. This is also case 2 in the well-known collection of kōans, the *Mumonkan.*

73. According to classical Buddhist thought, the fruit or results of karma can occur during three periods. Some karma bears its results in the present life, sometimes as soon as a morally charged act is performed. However, the effects of the act may not occur until the next life. In

some cases, many more lifetimes may lapse before the effects of the karma are felt. Thus, it may seem that sometimes the wicked flourish and the innocent suffer, but this is just the maturation of past good and bad karma.

74. The five unpardonable offenses are 1) killing one's father; 2) killing one's mother; 3) killing an arhat; 4) creating a schism in the Sangha; 5) causing a Buddha to bleed. There can be no expiation for these offenses, and the offender falls immediately into one of the drearier Buddhist hells.

75. Nāgārjuna is counted as one of the Indian ancestors of the Zen lineage.

76. Pu-tai is a fat, jolly character in dishevelled clothes, carrying a large, bulging sack, who is often portrayed in Chinese Zen paintings. He is the so-called "laughing Buddha" often seen in souvenir and gift shops. He is thought to have been a real person who was considered by the folk to be an earthly incarnation of Maitreya Buddha. It is interesting that here he is portrayed as a non-Buddhist.

77. Dōgen is alluding to the widely held view that the Buddhadharma had entered the last of three periods of change. The first period (often given as five hundred years) was supposedly the period of the authentic Dharma, during which time monks and nuns really practice hard and lead lives in accordance with the Buddha's teaching. The next period is called the period of the "counterfeit Dharma," when monks look like monks but do not really observe the teaching in a strict manner. The third period, called *mappō* in Japan, was thought to have started near the end of the eleventh century, and marked the utter collapse of the Dharma. At this time, there would not even be any pretense of following the Dharma, and it would be a period of moral, social, and religious degeneracy. Dōgen apparently accepted the theory of *mappō,* but he seems to have drawn different conclusions than Shinran, founder of Pure Land Buddhism.

78. The quote is from the *Lotus Sutra,* "Dharma Teacher" chapter. All references to "sutra" in this essay mean *Lotus Sutra.*

79. "Mark of ultimate reality that all things have" is a translation of *jissō,* sometimes translated as "true-mark" or "mark of reality" in other translations. It means that all things, just as they are, reveal the true state of reality, the body of the Buddha.

80. *Anuttara samyak sambodhi* means "supreme, perfect enlightenment." It is the enlightenment of Shakyamuni.

81. *Lotus Sutra,* "Life-Duration" chapter.

82. These are volume measures, a *koku* equaling almost five gallons, a *shō* equaling a little over one and a half quarts.

83. From the *Lotus Sutra*.

84. A pratyekabuddha is a person who is enlightened without the guidance of a master and who does not choose to share his understanding with others. Sometimes translated as "solitary Buddha," the pratyekabuddha is often found mentioned along with the arhat, who is also considered to be unwilling to mingle with ordinary beings and help them. Both the pratyekabuddha and arhat are thus examples of selfishness.

85. The three parts of the canon are: 1) the collection of discourses or sermons *(sūtra)*; 2) the collection of metaphysics or scholastic analysis of sutra terms and concepts *(abhidharma)*; 3) the collection of monastic regulations and codes of conduct *(vinaya)*. In other words, he knew all the vast collection of canonical literature.

86. The "three worlds" are the world of desire *(kāma-loka)*, the world of form *(rūpa-loka)* in which desire is absent or minimized, and the formless world *(arūpya-loka)* where beings are formless. According to ancient Indian Buddhist cosmology, they are arranged vertically, with the *kāma-loka* on the bottom containing the realms of man, animals, and the purgatories, as well as several classes of *deva* or celestial being.

87. The "eight liberations" are eight forms of meditation. They are liberations in the sense that one is freed from some form of bondage in each.

88. These are special kinds of knowledge belonging to one who has reached the rank of arhat. They are: 1) insight into the past lives of all living beings; 2) clairvoyance, especially with regard to the future; 3) insight into the cessation of impurity.

89. Fa-ch'ang was also called Ta-mei (after the mountain where he lived), which means "great plum." Ma-tsu was acknowledging his attainment.

90. A monk lived at the foot of a mountain by himself, where he dipped water from a stream with a long-handled dipper. For many years, he did not shave his head as a monk should. Once another monk visited him and asked him, "What is the meaning of Bodhidharma's coming from the West?" The monk replied, "The stream is deep, the dipper handle is long." When his master heard of this later, he thought it was a remarkable thing to say. Taking a razor, he went to visit the unshaven monk. He asked the monk if he had indeed said such a thing, to which the monk replied that he had. So the master told him that if he was able to teach, he should shave his head. So the monk washed his head and

knelt before his master, who then shaved his head. This story is recounted by Okada Gihō in *Shōbōgenzō shisō taikei,* vol. 3 (Tokyo: Publishing Bureau of Hozai University, 1953), p. 201.

Genealogy Charts
of Chinese Zen Masters

The following lineage charts have been included in order that the reader may be able to locate in time the various individuals mentioned in Dōgen's essays. I have made charts instead of a simple list so that not only a particular individual, but also his teacher and his own students, can be located. Several points need to be noted.

1. Asterisks mark a master who is not mentioned in the essays but who is included in the charts for purposes of clarity.

2. Dots between masters indicate that there is a break in the lineage and not all the individuals between the two are given. This is for the sake of brevity and simplicity.

3. "N.D." after a master's name means "no dates," because they are unknown.

4. Japanese pronunciations of names are given in italics following the Chinese names.

5. The double line traces the Ts'ao-tung (Sōtō) lineage of which Dōgen was part. I have traced the lineage from Ch'ing-yuan Hsing-ssu, but of course the lineage extends from him back through Hui-neng to Bodhidharma and beyond to the Indian masters.

Bodhidharma n.d.

Hung-jen
Kōnin n.d.

Hui-neng
Enō n.d.

Nan-yüeh Huai-jang
Nangaku Ejō d. 775
See next page for Nan-yüeh's lineage

Nan-yang Hui-chung
Nan-yō Echū 677–744

Yung-chia Chen-chüeh
Yōka Shikaku 665–713

*Ch'ing-yüan Hsing-ssu
Seigen Gyōshi d. 740

Shih-t'ou Hsi-ch'ien
Sekitō Kisen 700–790

*Yüeh-shan Wei-yen
Yakusan Igen 751–834

Tao-wu Yüan-chih
Dōgo Enchi 769–835

Chia-shan Shan-hui
Kassan Zenne 805–881

San-p'ing I-chung
Sambei Gichū 768–824

Yün-yen T'an-ch'eng
Ungan Donjō 782–841

*T'ien-huang Tao-wu
Tennō Dōgo 748–807

*Lung-t'an Ch'ung-hsien
Ryotan Soshin 782–863

Te-shan Hsüan-chien
Tokusan Senkan 782–865

Hsüeh-feng I-ts'un
Seppō Gison 822–908

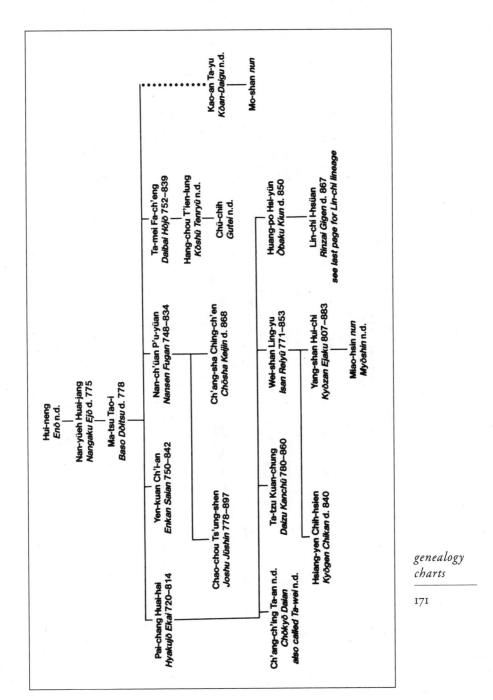

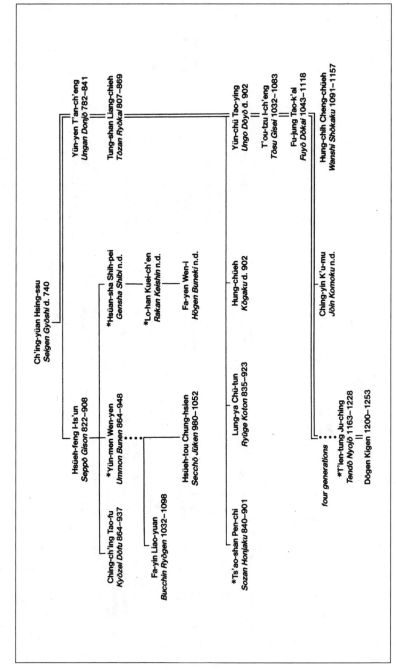

Ch'ing-yüan Hsing-ssu
Seigen Gyōshi d. 740

Yün-yen T'an-ch'eng
Ungan Donjō 782–841

Tung-shan Liang-chieh
Tōzan Ryōkai 807–869

Yün-chü Tao-ying
Ungo Dōyō d. 902

T'ou-tzu I-ch'eng
Tōsu Gisei 1032–1083

Fu-jung Tao-k'ai
Fuyō Dōkai 1043–1118

Hung-chih Cheng-chüeh
Wanshi Shōkaku 1091–1157

Hsüeh-feng I-ts'un
Seppō Gison 822–908

*Yün-men Wen-yen
Ummon Bunen 864–948

Hsüeh-tou Chung-hsien
Secchō Jūken 980–1052

*Hsüan-sha Shih-pei
Gensha Shibi n.d.

*Lo-han Kuei-ch'en
Rakan Keishin n.d.

Fa-yen Wen-i
Hōgen Buneki n.d.

Hung-chüeh
Kōgaku d. 902

Ching-yin K'u-mu
Jōin Komoku n.d.

Ching-ch'ing Tao-fu
Kyōzei Dōfu 864–937

Fa-yin Liao-yuan
Bucchin Ryōgen 1032–1098

Lung-ya Chü-tun
Ryūge Koton 835–923

*Ts'ao-shan Pen-chi
Sozan Honjaku 840–901

four generations

*T'ien-tung Ju-ching
Tendō Nyojō 1163–1228

‖

Dōgen Kigen 1200–1253

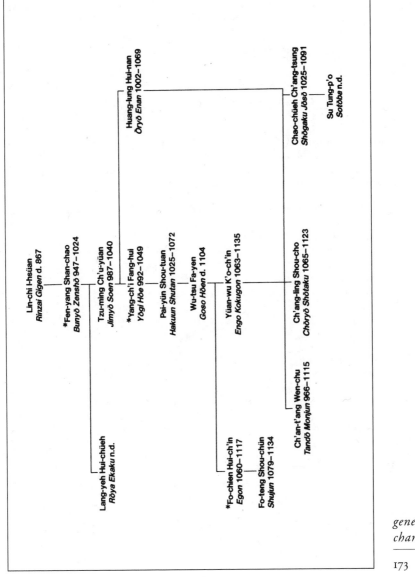

Lin-chi I-hsüan
Rinzai Gigen d. 867

*Fen-yang Shan-chao
Bunyō Zenshō 947–1024

Tzu-ming Ch'u-yüan
Jimyō Soen 987–1040

Lang-yeh Hui-chüeh
Rōya Ekaku n.d.

*Yang-ch'i Fang-hui
Yōgi Hōe 992–1049

Pai-yün Shou-tuan
Hakuun Shutan 1025–1072

Wu-tsu Fa-yen
Goso Hōen d. 1104

*Fo-chien Hui-ch'in
Egon 1060–1117

Fo-teng Shou-chün
Shujun 1079–1134

Yüan-wu K'o-ch'in
Engo Kokugon 1063–1135

Ch'an-t'ang Wen-chu
Tandō Monjun 966–1115

Ch'ang-ling Shou-cho
Chōryō Shōtaku 1065–1123

Huang-lung Hui-nan
Ōryō Enan 1002–1069

Chao-chüeh Ch'ang-tsung
Shōgaku Jōsō 1025–1091

Su Tung-p'o
Sotōba n.d.

Index

A
action vs. speech, 144–45
atonement/repentance, 20, 79–80

B
the bodhisattva, 32–33, 70–71
Buddha nature
  of all beings, 2–4
  obscured by self-oriented attitude, 9
  practice as manifestation, 3, 11, 19
  realized, 6–8, 9
  respecting other's, 11–12
Buddhism
  as experiential, 6
  faith defined in, 18–19
  goal of, 1, 50
  practice is, 2

C
cause and effect
  enlightenment related to, 40–42,
    45–46, 117–18
  heat of summer/cold of winter,
    40–41, 111–16
  karma and, 118–20
  Pai-chang and the fox, 45, 117–18
  the principle of, 123–24
  the reality of, 40–42, 45–46, 118–23
compassion, 31–34, 76, 79

conditionality and nonconditionality,
  84–86, 111–16, 162–48, 165–68
continuous practice (gyōji), 129–52.

See also practice
  components of, 129
  determination in, 135, 144
  examples in lives of the ancestors,
    131–37, 139–41, 147–52
  the freedom of, 138, 144
  inherent Buddha nature realized,
    6–8
  life and death within, 134, 145
  merits of, 129–30, 143–44
  need for in the Dōgen's Zen, 1–2
  neglecting, 130–31, 145–47
  of not leaving the monastery,
    137–38, 145
  the now of, 56, 130
  one day's importance, 130, 145–47
  ordinary life in, 10–13, 55–56,
    144, 147
  physical surroundings and, 141–42
  of raising an ox, 12, 136
  for the sake of continuous practice,
    149
  twelve austerities of, 131–32
  work's role, 135–36

D
desire
  enlightenment and, 7, 24, 35
  importance of eliminating, 24, 26,
    147
  and liberation, 104–5
  women as objects of, 104–5
Dharma

how to
raise an ox

About the Translator

FRANCIS DOJUN COOK was born and raised in a very small town in upstate New York in 1930. He was lucky to be an ordinary kid with ordinary parents. By means of true grit and luck, he managed to acquire several academic degrees and learn something about Buddhism. More luck in the form of a Fulbright Fellowship enabled him to study in Kyoto, Japan, for a year and a half, where he would have learned more had he not spent so much time admiring temple gardens. He now teaches Buddhism at the University of California, Riverside, and is director of translations at the Institute for Transcultural Studies in Los Angeles. He remains ordinary, but to his credit it can be said that he raised four good kids, has a great love for animals, and cooks pretty well. A sign that at last he is growing more intelligent is that he became a student of Maezumi Roshi several years ago, the best thing he ever did. He is also the author of *Hua-yen Buddhism: The Jewel Net of Indra,* and of various articles on Buddhism in scholarly journals.

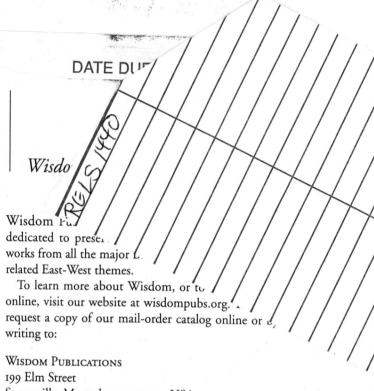

Wisdom Pu...
dedicated to prese...
works from all the major L...
related East-West themes.

To learn more about Wisdom, or to
online, visit our website at wisdompubs.org...
request a copy of our mail-order catalog online or 비,
writing to:

WISDOM PUBLICATIONS
199 Elm Street
Somerville, Massachusetts 02144 USA
Telephone: (617) 776-7416
Fax: (617) 776-7841
Email: info@wisdompubs.org
www.wisdompubs.org

The Wisdom Trust

As a not-for-profit publisher, Wisdom is dedicated to
the publication of fine books for the benefit of all and
dependent upon the kindness and generosity of spon-
sors in order to do so. If you would like to make a dona-
tion to Wisdom, please do so through our Somerville
office. If you would like to sponsor the publication of a
book, please write or email us at the address above.
Thank you.

Wisdom is a nonprofit, charitable 501(c)(3) organization affil-
iated with the Foundation for the Preservation of the Mahayana Tradition (FPMT).